祖母告訴我的故事

新秋的氣候，似乎比夏天還炎熱，晚間雖有微微風從破紙窗裏吹來，但被抱在祖母懷中的鳳寶寶（我的乳名）滿身都是汗，白天被母親用棍條打過的皮膚上，現着一條條的血痕，在銀白色的月光底下照出她的臉是慘白的，憂鬱的

忽然間，她由抽噎而放聲大哭了。

小乖，我的寶貝，你再不要哭了，哭醒了母親，她又會來打你的。

祖母說着恐嚇的話，輕輕地拍着寶寶入睡

A PAGE FROM THE ORIGINAL MANUSCRIPT

THE AUTHORESS IN UNIFORM

AUTOBIOGRAPHY OF A
CHINESE GIRL

■ **Dr Elisabeth Croll**, a Fellow of Wolfson College, Oxford and of the Oxford Queen Elizabeth House Centre for Cross-Cultural Research on Women, has studied both historical and contemporary women's movements in China. She is the author of numerous books on the subject, including *Feminism and Socialism in China, The Politics of Marriage in Contemporary China, The Family Rice Bowl: Food and the Domestic Economy in China* and *Chinese Women Since Mao.*

AUTOBIOGRAPHY OF A
CHINESE GIRL

Hsieh Ping-Ying

Translated into English by
TSUI CHI

With a new Introduction by
ELISABETH CROLL

PANDORA

LONDON, BOSTON AND HENLEY

First published in 1943
This edition first published in 1986
by Pandora Press
(Routledge & Kegan Paul plc)

14 Leicester Square, London WC2H 7PH, England

9 Park Street, Boston, Mass. 02108, USA

Broadway House, Newtown Road,
Henley on Thames, Oxon RG9 1EN, England

Printed and bound in Great Britain
by the Guernsey Press Co Ltd
Guernsey, Channel Islands.

Introduction © Routledge & Kegan Paul, 1986

Library of Congress Cataloging in Publication Data

Hsieh, Ping-Ying, 1906–

Autobiography of a Chinese Girl.
Translation of I Ko Nü Ping Ti Tzu Chuan.
1. Hsieh, Ping-Ying, 1906– – Biography.
2. Authors, Chinese – 20th Century – Biography.
I. Tsui, Chi.   II. Title.
DL2765.I.45Z46313 1986   895.1'8509 (B)   85–19260

ISBN 0-86358-052-1

CONTENTS

LIST OF ILLUSTRATIONS

In this *Autobiography of a Chinese Girl*, first published in 1936, a young Chinese student, soldier and writer recalls the details of her childhood, her school days, her army life and her relations with her grandmother, mother, brothers, sister and friends. In so doing, Hsieh Ping-ying has recorded her views on a wide range of subjects including her attitudes towards old customs such as bound feet and arranged marriage and on the modern life-style of a generation inspired by new forms of education, literature and political ideologies. It is the distinctive contribution of such personal documents as autobiography and diaries that they record one person's individual and often intimate perceptions of their times and thus greatly add to our knowledge and understanding of past events. For those whose gender and class have excluded them from the formal histories, they may be the chief means of documenting the details of their lives. For women, they offer an opportunity to make sense of the ways in which they perceive their own opportunities and choices, and expect these to be bounded by their families and by society. In times of rapid socio-economic change, they may provide the only evidence of the ways in which women respond to their changing and frequently fragmented environment, of the instances of female rebellion against old customs and of the individual circumstances surrounding the acquisition of new roles.

This is an illuminating set of memoirs for, despite some tantalising gaps, it vividly portrays the life of a young girl growing up at a time when traditional and modern and Chinese and Western influences jostled for supremacy in the minds of the literate and urban-educated young. The author was a young girl at a time when China had dethroned an Emperor and the once powerful Middle Kingdom was fast degenerating into an arena for competing warlords and foreign powers as they scrambled for political spoils and a share in the China market. It was also a period of cultural renaissance during which there was some fundamental questioning of traditional Chinese philosophies and customs and a widespread first acquaintance with new and powerful political and literary influences from abroad. Within the family it was a time when the ideal of romantic love was set against arranged marriage, agility and mobility were set against footbinding and seclusion and new forms of female education and occupation were set against domestic service and dependence in marriage. How to reconcile the individual quest for personal freedom and fulfilment with the old Confucian obligations on daughters and wives rooted in the traditional patriarchal family system was the central dilemma for modern young women such as Hsieh Ping-ying in the early decades of the twentieth century.

Hsieh Ping-ying, the youngest of five children, was either born in 1903 or 1906 (sources vary). As the second daughter born after a number of sons and into a household of a classical scholar, she escaped some of the discrimination suffered by girls born in less fortunate circumstances. Generally, daughters were welcomed into a family with less ceremony and fewer expectations than were sons and in the most extreme circumstances of poverty and dislocation, they might be the victims of infanticide or sold at an early age into domestic service or prostitution. In the competition for a share of scarce familial resources, daughters could not compete on equal terms with sons. Daughters did not perpetuate the family line or name and they could not participate in ancestor worship, provide economic support or enrich the family reputation through official appointment. The crucial fact was that 'a boy was born facing in and a daughter was born facing out' which only too accurately pointed to the transient nature of a daughter's life with her parents and the loss to her natal family on marriage. The poorer the household, the more the cost of daughters was counted, and one means of reducing the costs was to offer them as child brides to be brought up as adopted daughters-in-law in their future husbands' families. Hsieh Ping-ying describes the suffering of some of these daughters-in-law in her village who, unlike herself, had to pick tea to earn their keep. In contrast, in households such as Hsieh Ping-ying's where girls were less of an economic burden, they grew up and occupied an affectionate place in their families often learning something of books from their scholar-gentry fathers or sharing their brothers' tutors. However, although Hsieh Ping-ying was the 'little treasure' of her family and had been taught to read and write at her father's side, it was early recognised that she, like all daughters, was destined for another family.

Marriage in China was well-nigh universal and arranged by the family elders. Moreover it was frequently negotiated at the time of the children's birth or, as with Hsieh Ping-ying, soon after. The education of daughters was therefore exclusively designed to further their attractions as obedient and capable wives and daughters-in-law. As the influential *Classic for Girls*, which had for generations catalogued all the virtuous qualities of feminine conduct, made plain, 'You should study as a daughter all the duties of a wife'. It was the traditional obligation of mothers to instil in their daughters all desirable personal and practical attributes and their first duty to their daughters was the binding of their feet. Footbinding, a custom which for centuries had uniquely crippled the women of China, was still practised widely throughout China in the early years of this century although the first organisations had already been established in support of its abolition. The custom, first practised at court in the tenth century, had become associated with wealth and status, a symbol of femininity and virtue and an essential pre-requisite to the advantageous marriage so desired for all daughters. Matchmakers were reputedly asked not 'Is a girl beautiful?' but 'How small are her feet?'. Indeed, although a plain face was thought to be given by heaven, large or loosely-bound feet was said to be a sure sign of laziness or poor breeding. Hsieh Ping-ying's mother was like most aspiring mothers in that she herself, despite her own suffering, subjected her daughter to this painful process. Hsieh Ping-ying was fortunate to be the younger daughter in that her mother, learning from her error in binding her elder daughter's feet too tightly, delayed the binding of her second daughter's feet and was more lenient with her. Nevertheless, Hsieh Ping-ying describes here in graphic terms how she 'nearly died of pain' and how from one day to the next she lost her freedom and agility: 'The days of enjoying beautiful flowers and of catching fish and prawns would never come to me again'. Not surprisingly, relations between the mother who 'must bind her daughter's feet because she loved her' and the daughter who felt that her mother 'was no better than an executioner' were very strained at this time.

Personal documents written by women can give special entry to the secluded world of women; they provide insights on the relations between women of the same generation and, across the generations, reveal the intimate messages that are transmitted from grandmothers and mothers to daughters. In many respects it is the clash between the two strong and powerful personalities of mother and daughter which lies at the heart of this autobiography and prompts the author to reveal her innermost feelings and debates. Her mother is a good example of a Chinese woman of the older generation who might cite and instil the old adages of obedience, virtue and submission and at the same time exercise a degree of control and authority within the household which would be the envy of many a patriarch. Over the centuries the acquisition of power by women of the older generation through sheer force of personality, in the absence of or with the connivance of the men of the household had given rise to a powerful mythology of dominant mothers and mothers-in-law in China. This is despite the fact that women were denied any formal rights or voice in family or kinship affairs. In Hsieh Ping-ying's household, her mother was the dominant personality who had successfully controlled the lives of her three sons and first daughter. In the case of Hsieh Ping-ying, however, the conflict between mother and daughter was to be long and bitter and in the end irresolvable. It began in earnest with her desire to study, and after some altercation she was allowed to attend first the local village school for boys and later the Da Tung Girls' Mission School and the well-known Human Normal School for Girls located in the far provincial capital of Changsha. The strength of Hsieh Ping-ying's determination to depart from the traditional ways of seclusion, embroidery and marriage and go instead to school was evident from an early age, but only the extreme threat of suicide, the ultimate traditional weapon in the hands of young Chinese girls, enabled Hsieh Ping-ying to leave home and enter the new and modern world of the girls' schools.

During the first decades of the twentieth century it became more common and even respectable to send daughters to the new schools for girls. They had been established by either the government, missionaries or gentry women in the early years of the century with the avowed aim of giving girls a modern education so that they might become better wives and mothers. The schools were predominantly, though not exclusively, confined to the cities and treaty ports, and their pupils were largely drawn from the wealthy and leisured social classes who could both afford the fees and spare the labour of their daughters. In the history of the women's movement in China, these schools were very important new institutions not only because of the opportunities they furnished for female education, but because they took young girls out of the confines of their homes and away from the exclusive influence of their families and traditions. For the first time they were part of a much larger female constituency largely made up of their peers and their pioneering women teachers. For the first time, too, they came into contact with a new literature, the new ideas of women's emancipation and of individual and personal freedom and patriotic and nationalist causes. For this new generation of women, the new schools became the centres of a modern life-style. Another writer, Ting Ling, who attended the same school as Hsieh Ping-ying, has described the girls there as 'energetic, enthusiastic and unrestrained'. She recalled that as soon as they learned of a new idea they wanted to put it into practice. For instance, once the students learned of bobbed hair, they had a secret cutting session at which, despite the extreme prejudice against it, eighty students or so cut their hair. They had also felt deeply agitated over the future of China, and to show their concern they had gone out on the streets and wept over the humiliation of China at the hands of the foreign powers.

Hsieh Ping-ying, like Ting Ling, attended school during and in the aftermath of the May Fourth Movement which was one of the most exciting periods of youthful questioning and rebellion in twentieth-century China. During this very influential new cultural and literary movement, numerous papers and periodicals appeared which debated a wide variety of complex ethical and philosophic questions in the simpler vernacular of the people. Broadly, the aims of this movement were to discredit the old Confucian ideology and institutions and to introduce new social values based on the Western concepts of individualism, equality and democracy. The sources of many of the new concepts were Europe and North America and this was an age when foreign persons, ideas and literature enjoyed a certain popularity. To provide a forum for the discussion of the new ideas, young students like Hsieh Ping-ying's older brother began to publish their own magazines which were eagerly snapped up in the bookstores by the young. Many more students like Hsieh Ping-ying herself wrote articles and contributed their first literary efforts to these periodicals.

A particularly personal concern of these young urban literate students was the institution of arranged marriage. It had come to symbolise the 'domestic tyranny' of the 'ten thousand evil' Confucian society and the total lack of regard for the individual within the traditional patriarchal family. Most students had to look no further than to the experiences of their own brothers and sisters to see the 'unhappy fate' wrought by arranged marriage, and indeed this movement was notable for its ardent criticism and rejection of the Confucian family model. Romantic love and a brief romantic courtship based on the writing and receiving of love letters became an essential 'rite de passage' in joining the ranks of the modern young. There were few precedents to follow in establishing the new forms of courtship and free-choice marriage, and many of the letters and short stories published in the magazines arose out of writers' personal and often agonising predicaments in a transitional society. There is also evidence though of a new 'duty to society', and the new literature reflected the social concern among students and young urban professional workers for those less fortunate than themselves. Hsieh Ping-ying herself describes how she hurried back to school and penned a short story after witnessing the humiliation of a new slave girl at the hands of an insensitive employer.

In the new schools the girl students first came into contact with the concepts of nationalism and democracy, and it was the school communities of literate and articulate girl students which were among the main centres for patriotic activities. What particularly stimulated the students to act concertedly and organise collectively during this period was the Versailles Settlement at the end of the First World War which had allowed Japan to take over and occupy the old German concessions in China. This arrangement symbolised both the weakness of China to exercise sovereignty within its own national boundaries and the strength of the continuing and unremitting demands of foreign powers. The sense of national crises and the heightened patriotic and political consciousness brought many, including the girl students, into patriotic associations 'to save the nation' and on to the streets in demonstrations, boycotts and strikes. Even in Hsieh Ping-ying's school run by Norwegian missionaries, where the girls were refused permission to join the city parades, they refused to be excluded. At the risk of expulsion, they took matters into their own hands, wrote anti-foreign slogans on pieces of paper torn from their exercise books, pasted them on chopsticks and organised their own parades for the benefit of their teachers!

This period, while Hsieh Ping-ying was still at school, had seen both the height of Western influence in determining solutions to individual and national problems and also the beginnings of a new consciousness that the unity and strength of China might be dependent on the ousting of foreign powers. In the eyes of many of the young students, the bid to save their country was becoming increasingly urgent and the only group which seemed to offer some hope of uniting China and standing up to foreign demands was the new nationalist and revolutionary movement inspired by Sun Yat-sen. This new movement which had established its base in the southern city of Canton aimed at achieving a unified and independent China and a new society based on democratic principles. The Kuomintang Party, founded by Sun Yat-sen, and the newly established Chinese Communist Party entered into an alliance in 1923 to reunify China, and later in 1926 they embarked on a northwards march from Canton to the central valley of the Yangtze River as the first step in bringing the whole of China under one rule. However, this Northern Expedition, led by a new young military commander, Chiang Kai-shek, was more than just a military manoeuvre for it was also a carefully prepared and planned political movement to arouse peasants, workers and women in support of its wider socio-economic and political objectives. One of the platforms of the nationalist revolutionary movement was the emancipation of women and the Communist Party specifically called on women as one of a number of oppressed groups in China to support its goals. For this purpose some three to four hundred girl propagandists had been attached to the army. They had bobbed hair and wore the trousers, military jackets, belts and caps of soldiers but they did not fight. Rather they looked after the wounded and they organised women's and peasant unions in the wake of the moving armies.

As the expedition approached the city of Hankow, strategically located on the Yangtze River, the more radical elements of the nationalist revolutionary movement established a base there and began to recruit and train young men and women leaders to organise and work among women, peasants and workers. Soong Ching-ling, the young widow of Sun Yat-sen, later recalled how in Hankow she had been besieged by young students wanting to know how they could contribute to the new movement. To channel the energies of these eager but unprepared young students, a number of new schools for girl propagandists and leaders were opened to train them for military matters and educate them in the policies and aims of the new movement. It was at one of these, the Wuchang Central Political and Military School which offered a twelve-month course for girl propagandists, that Hsieh Ping-ying was finally enrolled. Like many of the other girl recruits, who like herself were mostly middle-school graduates, she initially entered the army as a means of escape from the imminent fate of an arranged marriage. At the time, Hsieh Ping-ying had welcomed her brother's suggestions that she enter the army for 'where could she go, a girl of under twenty years of age and without half a piece of cash to bless herself with'. Her priorities were transformed, however, once she put on her uniform and acquired a common sense of responsibility for the future of the 'more than one thousand million oppressed people of the country'.

In Wuchang Hsieh Ping-ying was one of twenty girl propagandists selected to travel with the army on its first expedition into nearby Honan province, and it was while she was on this march that she began to write her war diaries which were to make her a well-known figure in urban literary circles. Daily, either at mid-day rest or by the dim light of an oil lamp and using her knee as a writing desk, a 'wretched pen' and any scrap of paper she could get hold of, she wrote down the happenings at the front. These daily reports were published in the Central Daily Newspaper and they attracted a great deal of attention at the time. There should have been more, but as she noted in her autobiography, a bundle containing a second set of letters, her blanket, her water bottle and her food box disappeared at the front never to be found again. The first set of daily reports were collected together and published in her *War Diary* in 1928. The writer, Lin Yutang, who translated this first set of war diaries into English, describes how he met Hsieh Ping-ying in Hankow at this time. He recalls a very young, small girl with bobbed hair, who dressed in a grey uniform, talked and laughed in a hoarse voice. In a very easy and familiar manner she had entertained him and his friends with stories from the front as if she had known them all her lives and until the very roof seemed as if it 'was going to fall down on our heads'.

What is remarkable about Hsieh Ping-ying's records of thee years is not only that they are one of the few sets of surviving personal documents written by a girl soldier in the mid-1920s, but that they capture so well something of the vibrant sense of confidence, camaraderie and sisterhood which seems to have been generated by the single-minded sharing of a common belief in a new future and to have been a particular characteristic of the nationalist women's movement based in Hankow in the mid-1920s. There was a degree of excitement associated with the anticipation of a new era for women. A network of women's unions had been established and it was estimated that more than one and a half million women in over ten provinces were members of some kind of group linked to the nationalist cause. In the villages, towns and cities, the deliberate and hasty break with ancient customs such as bound feet, the appropriation of new symbols such as bobbed hair and the daring adoption of free-choice marriage and divorce separated these young women from the rest of the community and bound them into a heady solidarity. The rejection of these old values long revered by the rest of the community required courage, energy and mutual support. It was this spirit of independence, optimism and exhilaration which was widely commented on at the time and which characterises Hsieh Ping-ying's own account of her experiences. But as her autobiography also shows this period of confidence and optimism was short-lived.

Hsieh Ping-ying's account of how she and her fellow soldiers received the news that they were to be disbanded and demobilised is particularly poignant.For her, and for others, it marked an immediate transition from hope to despair and a period in which solidarity and confidence gave way to isolation and fears for their very survival. The abrupt change in fortunes in Hankow was caused by the rivalries within the nationalist movement which came to a head in 1927 when the more conservative Kuomintang Party embarked on a military offensive against the Communist Party and the more radical branch of the nationalist movement based in Hankow. One of the issues which divided the radicals from the conservatives was the role of the mass movements of peasants, women and workers. They were viewed by many with suspicion and hostility for they directly threatened the interests of the landlord, employer and banker supporters of the Kuomintang Party led by Chiang Kaishek. In 1927 the retaliation against anyone involved in these popular movements was swift and terrible and many young women activists lost their lives.

The open hostility and opposition aroused by the collective rejection of past prohibitions by the various women's unions was a potent weapon in the hands of the opposition. As is often the case in such periods of conservative reaction, the freedoms of women were singled out and cited in the most provocative of sexual imagery so as to give the impression that almost total licence and immorality prevailed in the areas influenced by Communist politics. Rumours and wild tales fell on willing ears and fed the wave of retribution which followed the split between the two parties. Women's units and unions were all closed down and, in the anti-Red reaction, any young woman with the tell-tale bobbed hair and a sunburned complexion was under suspicion. These were regarded as almost infallible evidence of radicalism, and on these pretexts alone thousands of young women were shot or killed after being subjected to gross indignities. Hsieh Ping-ying was one of the fortunate who escaped, although for the next two decades she was constantly harassed by the political authorities and frequently in fear for her own life. In the immediate aftermath of the Revolution of 1926–7, she returned to her native village. Without any alternative refuge or source of support she felt she had no other option but to return home and take up the cause of free-choice marriage within her own family.

Hsieh Ping-ying returned home in the full knowledge that she would have an enormous struggle to convince her parents to break off her betrothal which was considered to be as binding to the two families as if the marriage ceremony had already taken place. Other memoirs written by young men and women of the same generation suggest that for many the rejection of their childhood betrothal was the first serious instance of defiance against their parents' rule and authority and the first step in negotiating a marriage of their own free choice without parental interference. It was the important question of marriage which practically took the revolution or struggle between old and new practices directly into every gentry household and intimately affected relations between mothers and fathers and sons and daughters and brothers and sisters. As Hsieh Ping-ying's brother rather ironically suggested, it was easier to be brave on the battlefield than in their own home where with a mother like theirs they could not possibly expect there to be a revolution! For the lucky few, progressive parents co-operated with their sons and daughters to enable them to marry in the new way; others of independent economic means succeeded in disregarding the views of their parents altogether, but for the majority like Hsieh Ping-ying the conflict was bitter; and it was won by some and lost by many more. Hsieh Ping-ying knew that to have her own way would be difficult. Interestingly, at the same time as she was confident enough in the rightness of her cause 'to fight the old system with its own weapons and on its own ground', she was also sufficiently bound by old conventions to think that if her parents did not officially end her betrothal she could not with a clear conscience contract a marriage of her own choosing. Many of the new and modern young simultaneously subscribed to the new ideas and yet could not totally disregard the old conventions. Hsieh Ping-ying argued her case well, but her parents adamantly contested all her arguments in favour of free choice and marshalled all the established ideologies and forces of tradition in their support. Her mother was implacable in her opposition and challenged her defiance with all the weight of parental authority, charging her with ruining the family reputation, disgracing the ancestors and opposing the will of Heaven. Against this formidable array of opponents, Hsieh Ping-ying was without any very solid support from her brothers, sister or friends, let alone a women's union. Such family conflicts were a common feature of these decades, but they were still interpreted in terms of deviant individualism against an inviolable family unit, and without a well-developed analysis of oppression or organisation in support of the struggling individual, they often left the modern young isolated and exhausted and in the end defeated. In persisting in her opposition and attempts to escape, Hsieh Ping-ying was displaying the new spirit of perseverance supported by the student press which argued that to struggle was better than to take the traditional easy way out and commit suicide. But for many the truggle was too great and like Hsieh Ping-ying's friend, Shiang, they eventually admitted defeat and followed the old ways. Even Hsieh Ping-ying, who several times contemplated suicide, did not win the argument although she did escape from her home prison – only to find herself in a very different prison on the charge of being radical and Communist.

On her release from prison, Hsieh Ping-ying, like many other single young women of independent spirit but not means, turned to school-mistressing to support herself. In this first instance she was a reluctant recruit and she found the constraints of such a life barely tolerable. Indeed, within a very short time she found herself without a job and, with no prospect of a steady occupation or income, she thereafter embarked on what she called her wandering life. 'Like a wandering leaf in the autumn I would stay wherever I drifted to.' In the years after this autobiography ends and with the help of her elder brother, she did have the longed-for opportunity to study Chinese literature at university in Peking. But after two years she had to leave because of political harassment and the financial difficulties of supporting a former lover now in prison and her child whom she then reluctantly had to give up. For the next two decades she was to be constantly on the move travelling from city to city as she struggled to make ends meet as a part-time teacher, student, writer and editor. To make things more difficult, she suffered from persistent ill-health and she was frequently pursued by the political authorities in China and on her trips to Japan. On one occasion in Japan a whole second volume of autobiography was lost as she fled. When the writer Lin Yutang, who had earlier been so struck by her vitality, next met her in Shanghai he thought that her tragic fate was typical of that suffered by the idealistic young who were now hungry and broken in spirit by a world that had turned against them. When he met her she had escaped from marriage in her native village, had already been twice in jail and was now a 'derelict, persecuted by home and society' who was 'trying to support herself in the International Settlement by selling her writings at the rate of one to two dollars per thousand words'.

Despite all her hardships, she continued to edit various literary supplements and periodicals and to write herself, often penning several short stories a month under a number of different pseudonyms. In 1936 she completed the auto-biography presented here which she entitled *The Autobiography of a Girl Soldier*. Later, during the war with Japan, Hsieh Ping-ying devoted herself to mobilising women in support of the war effort. In 1937, as in 1927, she again accompanied the army to the front where she wrote of her experiences for the papers and these were later published as her *New War Diary*. After the war she continued to undertake a variety of teaching and editing jobs until 1949 when she left to teach and write similarly in Taiwan.

It is tempting to conclude that because of a combination of personal and socio-political factors Hsieh Ping-ying remained an adventurous if somewhat restless spirit who, although she won her personal freedom from the traditional constraints of family life, did not find so much of the personal fulfilment which she had sought in her youth. Indeed she hints as much herself during her only other visit home which is recorded in a short final chapter specially written in 1939 for Lin Yutang and his daughters who have also translated this autobiography. Four years after escaping from her home she had returned for a brief visit at the request of her mother and although there were no words of formal reconciliation, mother and daughter each secretly thought of the other in a more kindly light and silently suffered on the other's behalf. On one occasion during the visit, Hsieh Ping-ying's mother crept into her bedroom when her daughter was supposedly asleep and, patting the covers, murmured to her and shed tears over her daughter's thinness. As she went back to her room, Hsieh Ping-ying wished that she could go and kneel there to ask her forgiveness. She would not, but she does reflect then that perhaps she had let her mother suffer too much because she had wanted her freedom and her own life. She has a moment of self-doubt. 'Now what had I got after these four years of struggle. I had left the ancient way of marriage only to be entangled in romance. I wanted to tell my mother honestly, that I had gone through all kinds of suffering. I had been in prison. I had starved. I had given birth to a baby, I am still a persecuted refugee. My future is still dark.' However, she would not tell her mother these things for she thought 'they would hurt her too much'.

Her self-doubts may have lessened when she began to win acclaim for her writing. Although the room for her own writing was hard won, and she frequently wrote and wrote into the night to earn the desperately needed income, her name was frequently mentioned as one of the three foremost women writers of her day – alongside those of the better-known Ting Ling and Hsieh Ping-hsin. Although Hsieh Ping-ying wrote prolifically (she wrote under more than twenty different pen names), she is chiefly known for her war diaries of 1928 and 1939 and for her autobiography which is here translated by Tsui Chi. It was first published in England in 1943 and it is justifiably regarded as an important historical and literary record. It documents the individual struggle of a young Chinese girl to reject the traditional constraints and to gain autonomy and control over her own life. The fragments of rebellion, idealism and fortitude presented here reflect the struggles, hopes and exhilaration of a generation of student daughters during the first decades of the twentieth century and the poverty and persecution which often faced those cut adrift from traditional patterns and without familial support in the disrupted years that followed the first phases of the Chinese Revolution.

Elisabeth Croll
London, January 1985

目 次

Part One

MY CHILDHOOD

CHAPTER I

WHAT MY GRANDMOTHER TOLD ME

THE early days of autumn seemed to be even hotter than the hottest days of summer, although a tender breeze came incessantly from the courtyard through the broken paper lattice windows. The little girl, Phoenix Treasure—which is my milk name—was covered all over with perspiration. Earlier in the day I had been severely beaten by my mother with a stick, and even now there were distinct marks on all parts of my back. In the pale, soft moonlight my face must have appeared very pale and sorrowful.

Suddenly I started to sob again and eventually broke out into loud howling.

'My little Treasure, do not cry again. If your mother hears you, she will come and beat you once more.'

My grandmother, by using threats and soft words, tried to make me good and happy.

'I—I am not afraid of being beaten. Why doesn't she beat me to death?'

My voice was very loud, in order to provoke my mother. She was in the next room but she pretended that she did not hear me.

'My Treasure, you mustn't be naughty any more. You must know that your mother has suffered all kinds of difficulties on account of you. Remember when you once swallowed a piece of money which stuck in your throat and would neither go down nor come up. You appeared to be almost dead, and for a while your eyes were rolled backwards showing nothing but the whites, and water came trickling from your mouth. Your mother was nearly frightened to death. She had actually to tramp over a high mountain, which is a journey of twenty *li* [three *li* equals one mile], to get a doctor. She was almost crazy. She knelt down before the doctor and said, "If you can only save my poor child, I am quite willing to give my life for her." Later on the coin went down, and she was afraid that the copper would be absorbed into your blood and poison you. So she sent a special messenger to the city of Pao-Ching to buy a special kind of herb to cure you. Every time you went to stool she examined it very carefully to see if the coin was there.

'Another time you climbed to the top of the house to get at the nests of the swallows, and you fell down, breaking your head. You stopped breathing for a long time and became cold, remaining unconscious for a long period. Your mother cried incessantly. Sending for the doctor on one hand, she also knelt before the Goddess of Mercy and asked for some holy water to cure you. She said, " If my Phoenix Treasure is destined to suffer some calamities, please let them fall upon me instead, for I would willingly take them all. If only you protect her and make her healthy and lively, please take my life instead, or let all the calamities fall on me." These incidents you should really remember.'

I stopped crying and listened intently to what my grandmother was telling me.

'Alas, my Treasure!' she sighed and continued, 'you are really too naughty. I do not know what to make of you. Even in the very first months after your mother conceived you, whatever she ate made her sick. Even when she drank only a drop of water or ate a single green pea, she would be sick. She had headache and stomach ache. During the last two or three months she felt so miserable that she thought of committing suicide. But when she realised that she had three boys and another daughter besides you, all of whom she had to bring up, she thought better of it and carried on.

'When the time came for you to enter into the world, it was a matter of life and death for her. She began her labour two days before and could not rise from her bed. Apart from the fact that she could not eat any rice, not even a drop of water passed her lips. She rolled and tossed on her bed for two days, and then your little head began to make its appearance. I thought the baby would now be delivered at once, and full of expectation I was awaiting your arrival. But would you have thought that after a whole day and a whole night, all that could be seen was still only the little tuft of black hair on the top of your head! Your mother could carry on no longer and your father was not at home. I was the only one at her side and I dare not leave her for a moment, so what could I do? Later on your sixth great-aunt brought a midwife. Ah, when I remember the midwife, I feel furious. Your mother had had four children before you, and never once were we bothered with a midwife, and never had the labour lasted more than an hour when the baby was delivered. Who would have thought that this time, after so long a period of labour, you would still be undelivered! What do you think the midwife said to me? "There is no hope, you had better prepare the coffin." The beast, she was cruel to say such horrible things. "But the baby must be born at any cost . . . ," your sixth great-aunt said. "You must save the mother. If you have to sacrifice the baby, it doesn't matter."

'I felt hopeless. Your mother, who was always self-possessed, said to me through her sobs, "Mother, please pray to the holy god of the Sacred South Mountain. If the baby should be a boy I will send him on a pilgrimage to the holy god when he reaches the age of sixteen; and should it be a girl, then I will take her personally to the Great Mountain when she reaches the age of twenty."

'When I heard what she said I knelt down and prayed earnestly promising this sacred pilgrimage. Let god be praised, for at daybreak on the third day you were born crying. You had a very loud voice which had probably disturbed all the people in the neighbourhood. Your little eyes were like two brilliant lamps and you could roll them very rapidly. You shook your little fists and kicked incessantly. Your sixth great-aunt sighed and said, "What a pity that this is a girl. Had it been a boy I am sure he would have become a great official. Look at the quick-moving eyes."

'Your mother did not approve of her words and said: "What difference does it make whether it is a boy or a girl: they are the same to me." So you should know that your mother, although having suffered so much for your sake, loved you the instant you were born. My Treasure, from henceforth you must not annoy her, and you must remember her sufferings and her agonies for you.'

Though I was only six years of age I was quite intelligent, and could understand all my grandmother said. In my little mind I could picture to myself the sufferings my mother underwent when she gave me life. But curiously enough there was in my mind at the same time a deep impression of my mother beating me very severely on that same day. Above all, my little brain was working very quickly, and I had a suspicion that the remark attributed to my sixth great-aunt about sacrificing the life of the baby had really been made by my grandmother herself. But I knew my grandmother loved me very dearly and I had no intention of quarrelling with her. Above all, my life had not been sacrificed.

'A—Ahem! Since my mother loved me so devotedly, why should she beat me so severely? Are children not human beings? Should they not be allowed to think for themselves? Should they bow down to every little whim of the grown-ups?' These thoughts would keep coming in my mind.

Yes, I confess I was a very naughty child. I constantly caused my mother to be angry. But she was a dominating person, who could control quite a lot of the people around her. It was said that she could even control all the people, male and female, old and young, indeed everybody in my native village of Hsieh-To-San. But she could not control me—a little monster full of mischief! This was the only thing which annoyed her. Sometimes she was so desperate about me that she would say to my father, 'Please take her away from me for ever. This child does not belong to me.' Or she would say, 'Let us marry her off as early as possible and it will be a good riddance,' and so when I was only three years of age I was affianced to the son of one of my father's friends. When I was still a little baby in my mother's arms, my future was determined by the arrangements of other people.

Chapter II

MY FAMILY

My father was an only child, and he was born in most poor circumstances into the family of a farm labourer. This was what my grandmother told me about her marriage to my grandfather:

'Although my family was poor before I married your grandfather, your family was even poorer than mine. Even if there had been sufficient rice to eat, I do not think there was more than one bowl to put it in.'

'What do you mean, Grandma?' I asked.

'Well, let me tell you. Your great-grandfather had six sons, and your grandfather was the second. When your great-grandfather died, he bequeathed to each of his sons a very small portion of rice, one bench and one bowl, and that was the entire inheritance which your grandfather received. So you see that your grandfather had not more than one bowl to put the rice in. What could we have done if I had married your grandfather then?'

'You could have bought another bowl.'

'Yes, in a way. Your grandfather was an honest and diligent labourer at the farm, so his master was very kind to him. He earned a little money, and saved it all, so not only could he buy another bowl, but he was able to have enough money to marry me eventually. When I first married into your family I had to weave cloth and do all kinds of hard jobs for other people in order to earn our living. By and by we began to buy farm implements for ourselves, and from his former master your grandfather borrowed a little money to buy an ox. From henceforth we leased a few acres of land to plough and till. Alas, talking about ploughing and tilling I cannot forget the boyhood of your father. When he was only seven or eight years of age he gained an immense love of reading. Every day when he went to look after the cow he always took books with him. The moment he arrived in the open field he sat down and started to read, not caring whether the cow went astray and ate other people's wheat or cabbage or beans. He would not have cared even if the heavens fell.

'One day when he was reading the ox strayed, and he went crying in the fields all the evening, not daring to come home. When a neighbour found the ox for him and sent it back, your grandfather was very pleased and did not punish the boy for nearly losing so valuable an animal. He could see the boy was not born to be a cow-herd but a bookworm, so he decided to send him to school. He said that if your father were diligent in his studies he might even enter him for the State Examinations later on. When your father heard these words he was almost crazy with delight. He studied in the daytime and also at night. When there was no moon he would light a pine twig and hold it in his hand. Sometimes he was so absorbed in his book that he got his fingers scorched and burnt and would never notice.

'In the year of Shin-Chiu (1901) he went to the capital of the Province to attend his examination. He had no decent clothes for the occasion, and I had to give him my worn and ragged underclothes for him to wear beneath the new gown which I had made for him. Your grandfather had to carry the luggage for him, and in the inn where they stayed the inn-keeper thought your grandfather was your father's servant and would not even speak to him. Later on, when your father was successful in the examination and became a "Raised Personality," nobody thought that the baggage porter was the honourable father of a "Raised Personality!" '

I knew quite a number of stories about my father. When Viceroy Chang Chih-Tung established the Academy of Hunan and Hupeh, he went there to study. His thoughts after that were moulded entirely on those of Confucius and Mencius, and he liked to study the works of the Sung Dynasty scholars. He maintained that a wise and sagacious person should keep himself aloof from entanglements, and he kept away from politics all his life. During the end of the Manchurian period, the Viceroy of Kwantung and Kwangsi, Wei Wu-Chwan, recommended six scholars to attend a special Imperial examination on the subject of Economics. Five of them went, but not my father. He was an ardent advocate of the old system, and held that to one's father and mother one must be absolutely obedient. His filial piety to his parents excelled that of the Philosopher Tseng. To all other persons he was always gentle, humble, respectful and kind, so there was no one who did not like to be with him; but to his children, especially in those things concerning studies and dealings with other people, his instruction was on the strictest principles, even more so than a severe teacher. Otherwise he was very kind to us, and much more gentle and loving than our mother.

It is curious to think that, although he had the most old-fashioned brain I have ever known, there were a few new ideas which he did not oppose. For instance, when my second elder brother was studying English in his middle school days, my father encouraged him to pay as much attention to the foreign language as to his mother-tongue. He had been for twenty-seven years the headmaster of the Shin-Fa Middle School, and had engaged most of the masters to teach various scientific subjects, and all these men were graduates from modern colleges. 'Of course, on the other hand he was a great supporter of the classical language and a protector of the old moral code. So even when I was a tiny little girl spending most of my time in my father's arms, I was taught to read classical poetry and essays by old masters.

As for my mother, she had a very strong personality. She was a brave woman and was not afraid of anything in heaven or on earth.

Her mother had no sons but only three daughters, my mother being the eldest, and she was allowed to run the whole household at sixteen. After she married my father she became the most prominent figure in the village of Hsieh-To-San. She was extremely clever, and seemed specially endowed for managing affairs. In her mind she followed the old teachings of the 'three obeys' and the 'four virtues' of the model woman. (The 'three obeys' are to obey your father when you are a girl, to obey your husband when you are married, and to obey your children when you are a mother. The 'four virtues' are to be virtuous, to be discreet in your speech, to be tidy and to be diligent in your work.) She also had the fixed idea that the man is higher than the woman. She held the old-fashioned moral code dearer than her own life. In her own family and in her dealings with other people she was always the one to give the orders, which had to be obeyed. In fact, she was nick-named the Mussolini of Hsieh-To-San. All the people in the village obeyed and respected her. She also undertook to look after the public property of the village. She was a trustworthy person, absolutely honest and full of public spirit. In the management of the affairs of the village she was simply indispensable. If there was a question which could not be decided at the councils of the village, the only thing to do would be to invite my mother to their meeting, and after a few words from her the question would be immediately settled.

She was born with a resolute, or rather an obstinate, character. The people feared her and therefore would do her bidding. As she was the dictator of the village, naturally she was an absolute tyrant to her family; all her children were her slaves, and had to act exactly according to her instructions. Once when my eldest brother took his wife to establish a small family in the city of Yi Yang, about five hundred *li* from our village, not having obtained her consent before their departure, she immediately ordered them back, and my elder brother was severely punished by being made to kneel on the ground with a large basin of water balanced on his head. If he made the slightest movement the water would spill out of the basin and my mother would beat him for his negligence. It was only after the soft words of many friends to pacify her that she at last consented to forgive him.

My second elder brother was married to a fierce woman who had a pair of bound feet, and they did not love each other at all. When he wanted to have a divorce, my mother, striking the table, scolded him in a loud voice, calling him, 'You beast! after you have read the books of our sages, all you have learned is to suggest such a shameful, immoral proceeding! Do you not want to preserve the face of our ancestors? If you want to have a divorce, you must kill me first. Until I am dead never dare to think of such a disgraceful thing.'

My second elder brother knew only too well the determination of my mother. If there was a divorce, it was most probable that a death would occur in the family, so he had to go on suffering until he died by spitting blood. He led a very lonely life, and never dared to approach a second woman.

As for my sister, she was as tame as a mouse. Before her mother she dared not even to speak aloud. At eighteen she married a man by the name of Liang. Of course the match was of my mother's choice. In the Liang family her husband and her father and mother-in-law were very cruel to her, but when she came home she pretended she was well treated. She knew that if she acted otherwise she would get no sympathy from our mother, who would naturally upbraid her for being undutiful as a wife. When we met privately in the lavatory she would shed tears before me and tell me all her sufferings. I also heard her cry in her sleep when she was staying with me.

My third elder brother had also to be obedient, but he could manage his affairs better, and sometimes even dared to oppose our mother's orders. Sometimes he could contrive a very clever plan to get what he wished done. As for myself, I am ashamed to confess I was just a rebel.

CHAPTER III

THE GOLDEN DAYS OF MY CHILDHOOD

I WAS by far my mother's youngest child because my sister was ten years my senior. She married when I was only eight years old. Of my three elder brothers, two of them went with my father to study in the city of Shin-Fa. Soon my eldest brother became a teacher, and they would all come back twice a year.

The winter and summer vacations were times for the whole family to meet. In the early days of the winter every year my mother would prepare a lot of dried fish and salted pork in anticipation of their happy return. I envy the kind of holiday life which my father and brothers enjoyed. Every time we received my father's and elder brothers' letters saying they would be home on such and such a day we would be so happy that we could not sleep on the one or two nights before their arrival. My mother would cook a splendid meal and make me change into my best dress, and she would say, 'My Treasure, do not soil your new clothes. Father will bring you sweets and your elder brothers will bring you toys.'

It is about ninety *li* from the city to our home, and there are two steep mountains to be crossed. Father used to come home in a sedan chair, and there would be a porter carrying the luggage. My brothers would be dressed in their short jackets and wearing straw sandals. Following father's sedan chair they had to trot very quickly and would be panting all the time. Sometimes my mother would take me by the hand and stand outside the door waiting for their return. From the late afternoon till about twilight we waited, and at last, when we could see the top of the sedan chair approaching from the distance, she would say, 'My Treasure, your father has come home!'

While my mother went into the house to prepare boiling water to make tea, I would run racing with a tiny black dog to greet my father half a *li* from the house. As a rule my father would not be in his sedan chair by that time, because about eight *li* from the house he would get down and walk, the reason being that from that point onwards were the graves of our ancestors, and after that the houses where some of our elders were living, and it would be contrary to the proprieties if he passed these venerable places in a sedan chair.

'Father, where are the sweets?'

Like a little monkey climbing up a tree I would climb up my father and hold tight to his shoulder, and the little black dog also would wag his small tail and jump up at my father. When my second elder brother would try to drive the dog back, striking him with a stick, my father would say hurriedly, 'Don't drive him away, don't drive him away. He is just like Treasure and only wants to welcome us home.'

They would all smile. Even the porter who was carrying the luggage would grin. But I was not amused and pouted my lips. I did not like my father comparing me with a little dog.

There were times when I went to greet my father and he would carry me home. In the winter he would wrap me in his fur coat, fearing that I would catch cold. As soon as we entered the house my brothers would give me all the toys they had brought with them, and many of them had been made by themselves, such as little boxes, stuffed sparrows, little boats, and penholders. Then there were glass bottles of blue ink and glass tubes and pipes which they took from the chemical laboratory. The things I liked most were the glass test-tubes. In summer I would catch fireflies to put in them, and in the dark when they moved about, upwards and downwards in the tubes, they looked like golden dragons wriggling and sparkling, and were very lovely indeed.

Father would buy nice things for grandmother to eat, as well as buying me some of a special kind of pretty little buns which had pepper in them. Mother was always afraid that I would give all of them to my playmates, so she always kept them for me, only giving me a few at a time. However, I was not to be outdone by her. Unknown to her I would get some sweets from my grandmother, and then run out of the house and distribute them among my friends.

For this purpose I had to have a big pocket in my coat, and once, finding that one of my coats was not provided with such a pocket, I refused to wear it until one was added. Because I was so obstinate my mother hit me with a stick, and I had to run away. As she had tiny bound feet and could not catch me, she shouted

'Stop!' but instead I ran all the faster, and suddenly I heard her fall down into the water of the rice fields. As it took some time for her to get out of the muddy water, I took the opportunity to run back into the house, asking my elder sister-in-law to save me. Of course she could do nothing, and soon my mother came back, locked me in a dark room and beat me severely with a stick. It was on the night of this occasion that my grandmother told me about my mother and, because I was bruised all over, I slept with my grandmother that night.

My father liked to plant flowers, and in our little garden we had flowers of all colours and at all seasons, and also fruit trees of all kinds, such as oranges, pears, plums, peaches and *pipa*. There were also green bamboos and grey pines. When the roses were in full bloom the garden looked very lovely, and the finches would come there and sing all day long. I spent many happy days in this paradise.

When my father was at home he would always spend his days in the garden, weeding the lawn or watering the plants. At night he would teach us to read classical essays and poems, while my mother and sisters-in-law would be working at the spinning-wheel. Sometimes the gentle sound of the spinning-wheel would linger in harmony with the poems which my father was humming, and it became a kind of intoxicating music to me. On many such occasions I fell asleep in my father's arms, and on the following day when he asked me to recite the poems he had taught me on the previous evening, I could not do so and would say blushingly:

> 'Little Treasure was in father's arms,
> And Little Treasure soon went to sleep.'

'Who taught you to say that poem?' My father looked angry but I knew he was only pretending, and could see a little smile just at the corners of his lips.

'Little Treasure taught it to herself.' Saying this I flew away like a little sparrow.

When spring came to our village, lovely grass was all over the fields. Red and white flowers bloomed everywhere. Gentle ripples whispered in the streams. The birds began to sing their spring song incessantly. This was just the time for the farmers to plant their rice and for the children to start catching their fish and river prawns. In our part of the country it was always drizzling with rain in the spring, and the farmers wore their palm-leaf water-proofs and worked with bare feet in the rice fields from morning till dark. When I saw people coming home carrying small fish, I knew it was time for me to go out and do the same.

I would act just like the boys, taking off my socks and shoes and going out in the rain with a bamboo-leaf waterproof hat on my head. My playmates were all very naughty boys, and we went wading in the dirty shallow water, trying to catch prawns and fish. Sometimes, when the water in the brooks was running too rapidly to enable us to catch any fish there, the boys would plan to go into the rice fields and steal the farmers' fish, for the breeding of fish is the secondary industry of the farmers in our part of the country. But I did not care so much for fish as I did for prawns and crabs, neither did I want to be a thief. I also liked field snails, but while picking up these things I was often bitten by leeches. Whenever I came home crying because of leech bites my mother would upbraid me very severely, and she had good reason to do so. I would be wet through and covered with mud.

'You know you are a girl, why do you mix with those naughty little brats?'

'Why cannot a girl go out and play in the fields?'

'She just can't. She must stay at home!'

Then I would have a good thrashing, and my mother's angry voice and my howls would fill the house.

CHAPTER IV

TEA-GIRLS AND SPINNING-MAIDENS

BECAUSE I was so naughty and would not stay at home in the day-time but played in the fields, my mother punished me by assigning to me a kind of hard labour. Every day after breakfast I had to go to the tea-garden to pick tea-leaves. It is about two *li* from my home to the tea-garden and I could not come home for my lunch. My mother would send a man to bring me lunch in a little basket. My sister-in-law and I, with a number of tea-leaf picking girls, worked in the garden all day until dusk.

I had no experience of tea-leaf picking, and I would pick the branches of the tea trees. My sister-in-law was greatly worried and said:

'Younger sister, you had better go and catch butterflies instead of ruining all the tea plants. If your mother knew about this you would not get off lightly.'

'But I want to pick tea-leaves. Nobody was born to pick tea-leaves. One has to learn.'

My sister-in-law was rather talkative, but when she was working with me I always made it impossible for her to answer me back.

Although my job was to pick tea-leaves, it would be better to describe my work as picking flowers. Every time when I was on my way home my little basket would be full of wild flowers. When I came to the very long span bridge I would throw all the flowers over the bridge into the water, to be carried into the Tung-Ting Lake. I would say a word of farewell to them:

'O flowers, go to the Dragon King whose daughter is soon to be a bride and must be decorated properly.'

When I was very young, a carpenter who was making furniture as part of my sister's trousseau told me that the Dragon King's daughter was the most beautiful girl in the world, and was still unmarried. If the day of her wedding arrived the whole earth would be overwhelmed with floods, and all the people on the earth would be floating in the water. I would have liked to see the whole earth covered with water, so I was constantly hoping that the Dragon King's daughter would marry very soon.

Most of the tea-leaf picking girls were what we call 'child daughters-in-law.' Their life was full of misery. Every day they had to pick at least forty or fifty *catties* of tea-leaves (a *catty* is a little more than a pound), and their wages would be only ten or twenty coppers a day, which they had to give to their mothers-in-law. If they were found to be keeping any of the money for their private use they would be severely punished. Rarely did they have a good meal. What they had was either small sweet potatoes or very coarse wheat dumplings. Except at the New Year's Festival, they could never hope to taste a slice of meat. They were as thin as skeletons, and when they went into the tea-garden they would exchange stories of the sufferings their mothers-in-law inflicted on them, and their tears would drop on the tea-leaves, glistening there like the dew of the early morning.

'If you are suffering from these cruelties, why do you not run away?'

I said this to a little girl who had bruises all over her. Her name was Spring Fragrance.

'Escape! How dare I? My mother betrothed me and sent me to my mother-in-law, in whose house and in whose hands I must die.'

She was so sorrowful that I shed tears for her fate.

'There is no use crying. You had better hurry on with your work. By the end of the day if you haven't done any work you will be punished with a severe thrashing. Why should you?'

Another girl, who was slightly older, and whose name was Talented Flower, gave her this kind of comfort.

'Alas! my fate is a miserable one! My life is even worse than that of the ox or the horse. But if I have suffered so much during this existence, I hope I shall have a better fate in my next one.'

Her eyes were already swollen with crying, and she tried to comfort herself in this way.

From now on I began to realise that there were other sufferings besides my own. I felt very sorry and angry at the lot of these poor child daughters-in-law, and in the tea-gardens I always tried to help them picking tea-leaves instead of doing my own work.

When dusk came we put away our tea-picking knives and benches, and shouldering our tea-baskets we sang this ballad:

'During the third moon the tea-leaves are grown;
Sisters begin to embroider their handkerchiefs.
On each side they work a tea flower,
And in the middle a tea-picking boy.'

The gentle autumn wind wafted in the subdued fragrance of the cassia. Our elder sister the moon was displaying her pure soft brilliance. Our playmates the stars were winking at us from the sky, and the children were playing in the open, either having a race with their own shadows or at blind man's buff. But I was not one of them. Though only eight years of age, I began to tackle the work of the grown-ups.

In the bright moonlight, beside myself and my sister-in-law there were two cousins and a girl from the next house, all spinning together.

All the girls in my part of the country were taught to spin cotton thread and to make hempen thread and do needlework at the age of seven or eight. The poorer girls worked for other people and their wages would be two hundred pieces of cash for a *catty* of cotton thread. The quickest spinner could at most do four ounces a day, average workers doing no more than two to three ounces. In this way their wages actually amounted to two or three coppers a day. I was spinning on my own and for myself, and so it did not matter how much I could do. My mother said:

'You do as much as you can at first. If the cotton raised by ourselves is not sufficient for you to spin, we can buy some more from the market at Nan-Tien.'

'No, I don't like spinning. I cannot possibly wear so much cloth.'

'You cannot wear all of it now, but you must prepare for your trousseau. If you spin very diligently it will enable you to send twenty cases of dresses to your future mother-in-law's home. What a good showing that will be!'

Though I knew at that time that I had been betrothed when I was still at my mother's breast, I could not understand what it meant, and had no idea of its absurdity. When I heard what my mother said I became happy and went on cheerily with my spinning. In the bright moonlight the work seemed to be rather enjoyable, but in winter time, when we were doing it indoors, it was not so good. For instance, in order to save light we had to spin by the fire. Then the atmosphere and the dim light made us miserable, and we did not have enough exercise to warm ourselves.

The weather in autumn was invariably good and the moonlight seemed to be specially pure and brilliant. Then grandmother would tell us stories, such as the love story of the Cow Herd and the Weaving Maid, the story of the Goddess of Heaven, and so on. Sometimes we became so interested in the stories that we stopped our spinning to listen, and we would ask her, 'And then what happened?'

'What happened? Well, all the lazy-bones stopped working.'

This unexpected conclusion made up by my grandmother made us all laugh.

The gentle sound of the spinning-wheel in the quiet and far-advanced night sounded very much like the notes of the lute coming from an empty mountain valley, and as the soft breeze wafted the fragrance of the cassia to us we felt intoxicated.

CHAPTER V

MY FIRST SUFFERING

MY mother began to hear things against me from outside. It was said that as I was growing up and my feet were still unbound it was most probable that my future mother-in-law would refuse to accept me. Moreover, it was scandalous to see a girl mixing with boys and playing at making mud pies, throwing stones and playing at commanders and soldiers. They maintained that, according to the proprieties of ancient times, children after four years of age must be separated, and boys and girls should not occupy the same table, and that my mother, being a well-educated woman, should realise the importance of these rules.

My mother had left me alone. She knew that her own small feet were bound too tight, so that it was very inconvenient for her to walk. My elder sister's feet were likewise bound very small. Though they looked very nice, she could not walk more than two steps without having to support herself by holding on to the wall. Indeed, my poor sister was no better than an invalid. My mother had decided to delay the binding of my feet so that I could walk better than my elder sister. In the meantime, however, she thought that if she did not start to bind my feet now, my bones would become hardened and there would be no likelihood that I would ever be able to have small feet. According to the custom of my country, girls with big feet would not be welcomed by those looking for daughters-in-law, and anybody who saw such a girl would exclaim: 'Her mother must have died when the girl was young. With a pair of feet as big as palm-leaf fans it is really ugly.'

When my mother wanted me to make a pair of small shoes to be put in front of the altar of the Goddess of Mercy I did not realise what this was for.

'My Treasure, to-day I am going to bind your feet. You go and kneel down before the Goddess of Mercy so that she will bless you and make you to have a pair of small feet.'

Holding incense sticks in her hand and burning silver-paper ingots, she asked me to kneel down.

'I don't want to bind my feet,' I said, and dare not go near her. Two tear-drops as big as peas fell from my eyes. In my mind I began to fear that suffering was waiting for me.

'Come quickly, come quickly! The Goddess of Mercy will relieve your pains.'

She came over and dragged me to kneel down on the ground.

Alas, everything had been carefully prepared. A pair of small shoes embroidered with two plum flowers, and two long pieces of cloth about three inches wide, the sight of which made me shudder, were placed before me. Though this pair of shoes was made of vermilion silk, had very thin soles and was very pretty indeed, I did not like it. Evidently mother had made this pair of shoes behind my back, because I had not seen her making it.

'Mother, it will be very painful. I won't be able to walk. Please do not do it to me,' I pleaded in tears and full of fear.

'I must bind your feet because I love you. If I do not bind your feet I shall not be doing the right thing by you. You must realise that a girl with huge feet will never be accepted by a husband.'

When my mother said this she sipped some water, which was said to be holy water and supposed to have been given to her by the Goddess of Mercy. Then she blew it out on to my feet and started to bind them. Of course I began to howl and struggle.

'Oh, Mother, I am dying of pain! I had rather never marry all my life than have my feet bound!'

'You little wretch, what is the use of howling and struggling? I will bind your feet the tighter for that.'

While she was binding my feet I kicked as hard as I could, and with my hands I tried to snatch away the cloths and to throw the shoes away. My mother was very angry and called out to my sister-in-law to take hold of my hands. Putting my right foot under her seat, so that I could not kick with it, my mother held my left foot very tightly and made a very good job of it. I, like a condemned prisoner who was going to be beheaded, shouted and howled, hoping to get people in the neighbourhood to come to my rescue. My sixth grand-aunt came, and the moment she entered our house she said:

'My Little Treasure, do not cry. After you have bound your feet I will carry you on my back to see the monkey show.'

I felt that all the grown-ups were hard-hearted, for not one of them had any sympathy for me, and my heartrending cries were of no avail. Alas, they were all like my mother, no better than executioners.

When I had put my new vermilion shoes on, not only my feet but my whole body felt rigid and numb. My mother planted me on the ground to try whether I could walk. I felt as if the bones of my feet were broken and I cried and fell down on the ground.

From henceforth I spent most of my days sitting by the fire spinning. Sometimes I could manage to walk very slowly in the hall. It seemed as though my feet were fettered, and to walk was very difficult. The days of enjoying beautiful flowers and of catching fish and prawns would never come to me again.

On the day of the Flower Festival, when I was still asleep in my bed, my mother pierced a hole in the lobes of my ears. The pain awakened me from my dreams, and I found two pieces of red thread looped in my ears.

'Well, of the three important things, I have done two of them for you,' my mother said very triumphantly.

What she thought to be the three important things for a girl were first to bind her feet, second, to pierce her ears, and third, to marry her off.

'Yes. There only remains one thing to do, and that is to kill me,' was my angry reply to her, which resulted in my having a severe scolding.

When my elder sister was married, my mother borrowed a lot of money to give her daughter a good trousseau. She engaged embroiderers to make sixteen pairs of lovely coverlets for her. There were seventy-two people to carry her furniture to her new home, and there were also eight big cases of dresses, shoes and stockings, every one of which had been embroidered.

My elder sister had started to embroider when she was only eight, and she seldom left her room, but worked all the time, and when she was eighteen she was married. In her tiny room, from six o'clock in the morning until six o'clock in the evening, she did nothing but embroider. In the evenings she had to spin. My poor elder sister, even when she was very weary and panting, would not dare to say anything about it to her mother. All she did was to sigh in secret.

Of course my mother wished that I would be like my elder

sister, doing a lot of embroidery work, so that by the time I married my trousseau would be very attractive. But I said to her:

'I don't want any of these things. All I want is to study.'

'Oh, a girl wanting to study? Really, the heavens will fall and the earth crumble! To study is the work of your elder brothers. You were born to be confined to your boudoir. Just think, what is the use of a woman who has studied? You know that there is no State Examination for women candidates.'

Though she opposed me in my request to study, it eventually turned out that I was to be allowed to go to the school.

CHAPTER VI

THE VILLAGE PRIVATE SCHOOL

MY native village was in an out-of-the-way, backward district, surrounded by peak after peak of mountains. A little river flowed by, and its ripples produced a melodious music all the year round. In the spring, when I opened my window I could see lovely blue sky, green mountains and beautiful flowers and trees, and now and again I could see birds flying here and there. Indeed, this was a closed-in village, with delightful mountains and a pleasant river, quite like a land of immortals.

There were about two hundred people in the village. The chief industry of the men was farming, while the rest were coal-miners. Shin-Fa was a coal-producing district of China, and the lead mine in our mountain was famous for its lead production.

The coal-miners spent their lives underground, in the day-time as well as at night. Not only was their skin blackened by the coal, but also the insides of their nostrils, their ears and their mouths, so that their sweat, their tears and their saliva were also black. The gentry of this village looked down on these people and gave them the name of 'Black Insides.'

And in our village all the women's feet were the famous three-inch-long ' golden lilies.' The poorer ones were generally sent away to be child daughters-in-law. Even the better off ones were married at fifteen or sixteen. Their daily work, besides looking after their houses, cooking, washing, mending, and bringing up children, was to help their husbands in digging, weeding and planting. But they were not allowed to go into the coal-mines because it was said that the coal-miners did not wear anything in the mines, so these were a forbidden quarter for the women.

All the girls in this village naturally would never dream of going to school. Though there was a private school only half a *li* from my home it was specially for boys, and the girls were not allowed to pass its threshold.

When I was only five years old I had begun to read. My father was a classical scholar—he has written more than thirty books—

so whenever he came home for the winter or summer holidays from his school he would teach me to read poetry.

I must confess that although I could recite these poems very fluently, I did not really learn all the words, and I could not possibly understand what they meant. It was much more like repeating nursery rhymes, such as 'The bright, bright moon,' after my grandmother, when I repeated the poems after my father. At eight I could recite most of the poems of *The Three Hundred Verses of the Tang Poetry*, and *The Poems by Girl Students of the Shey Garden*. After that the words I learnt began to increase, and my mother taught me to read *The Proper Rules for Bringing up a Daughter*, the *Biographies of Distinguished Women* and the *Women's Classics*. Strange to relate I couldn't understand why I never liked these books. When my mother taught me these things I felt they were dry and meaningless.

I began to ask my mother to send me to the private school, but she said girls need not go to school. If they could read many words and learn many stories of the *Distinguished Women*, if they could keep books and read title-deeds, that would be quite enough. Evidently she was hoping I would make a very good housekeeper, but I had a different ambition. After my repeated requests, she at last consented to send me to the private school when I was ten years of age. I never thought that a girl's ambition to study would meet with so many obstacles. Not only was the teacher reluctant to accept me as his pupil, but also those people who had nothing to do with us or the teacher protested against it.

In my native village they had never seen a girl going to school, and what was worse was that I was to enter a school for boys. My greatest enemy was a woman with a snub nose who had the nickname of 'Sharp-mouthed Grandma.' She was well known in the village as a cattish woman. Her only son was studying in that private school, and so when she heard that I was going to it she went out everywhere spreading tales about me. She said that if girls were allowed to go to the same schools as boys, then the wisdom of the boys would be stolen by the girls, and the boys would become stupid dolts. Then she condemned my mother as being ignorant of the proprieties. She said that girls and boys should be separated was well known by everybody; how could it be allowed for me, a nearly grown-up girl, to go to the boys' school? Although people were sympathetic to her, all they could do was to talk behind my mother's back. They were so afraid of my mother that none of them dared to approach her to stop me from going to the school. The 'Sharp-mouthed Grandma' was the bravest of all. She said she was afraid of nobody, so she came to see my mother and asked her not to send me to the school. She suggested that my mother should engage an elderly teacher to teach me in my home. She would rather see the school disbanded than see me go into it.

This was all to the good because my mother was of a very perverse nature. At first she had not been quite keen on sending me to the school, but after this interview she was more determined than anyone to send me there immediately. Having upbraided the 'Sharp-mouthed Grandma' very severely, she took the necessary stationery, together with incense sticks and silver-paper ingots which were to be used to worship Confucius, and took me to the school at once. As the teacher knew that my mother was the most authoritative person in Hsieh-To-San, he dared not say half a word about refusing me, though in his heart of hearts he was not at all willing to take me. He told my mother that he was greatly honoured to have a girl student.

After I had knelt down four times to the picture of Confucius, then twice before my teacher, which was the indispensable ceremony at the entrance of a new student, I was initiated into the school.

My teacher was a very short-sighted man. He had to press his nose almost on the book when he was reading. If the book happened to be printed in small type, such as the *Book of Confucius* and the *Book of Mencius*, he had to rub his nose incessantly on the book. A most repellent thing about him was that he was a very dirty man as well, and his book was stained with saliva from his mouth and drops from his nose. Nor were the students' books free from such pollution. Sometimes when he realised that it was too much, he would wipe the wetted books with his sleeves. But such good intentions were not appreciated by his students, and he was nicknamed by them 'The Filthy Blind One.'

His bed was in our classroom, and his bedclothes were as black as if they had come from the coal-mine. His bed was never in order, and sometimes a repugnant smell would assail our nostrils and make us nearly sick. We used to say among ourselves that he ought to have a bath because we thought he had never had one since his mother bathed him as a child, but we never dared to say this to his face, which was always a horror to us.

As I was a girl, so my seat was in front of the forty odd boys. My desk was nearest to that of the teacher, so every morning when the boys had to recite their lesson of yesterday they had to stand in front of me. Whenever a boy had any difficulty with his recitations I would oblige him by giving him a little help, which, though making me very popular with the boys, caused me some very severe scoldings from the teacher.

During the first year I finished eight books of *Girls' Readers*, a book of *Women's Four-character Classics*, and I secretly learnt half a book of *Familiar Quotations* and the *Book of Confucius*. Not that I could understand the meaning of any of these books at that time, because the teacher never explained the books to us, but I learnt like a parrot. The teacher praised me very much to my mother for my wisdom, but he immediately followed the words with a deep sigh.

'What a pity she is so naughty!'

Naturally my mother was not very pleased with this, but she said nothing. She hoped that if I should play truant or did not like to study, she would have a very good excuse for stopping me from going to the school.

I loathed this teacher more than the boys did, because in general a girl is used to being more tidy than a boy. For instance, their books were often very dirty, while I always tried to keep mine in a new condition. Besides the vermilion marks made upon them by the teacher's brush, I wanted to see no trace of a stain of any kind in my books. The great pity was that every time I had to hand my book to the teacher, he would leave some personal marks from his nose or mouth upon it.

'Please, teacher, please ask the doctor to look at your nose first before you give me my lesson.' Once I was so bold as to make this suggestion to him.

'What are you saying?' He looked up and roared at me.

I was frightened, but all my schoolmates started to laugh.

One evening in the early summer, when a heavy shower was just over as our lesson was finished and he was going out, I planned to do some mischief as a revenge for his having dirtied my new book. After the rain everything was running with water, and there were big pools here and there in the street. In the open fields there were several places where the water was as deep as in the rice fields. My schoolmates were playing at sailing boats on the water by using bamboo leaves as sails. Some of them were catching prawns and little fish, and they were all very happy. As they were all busily engaged in their own pursuits I was preparing to do some mischief.

Just before we went home the teacher was punishing one of the students by beating the palms of his hands, and all the other boys were kept in to see the punishment. I stole away and got a tray of sawdust, spreading it on the surface of a pool of water in the middle of the road leading from the back door of the school. I then went back to the school and replaced the tray. Very soon the students were dismissed and all began to go home. The teacher locked the door of the schoolroom and was on his way out by the back door to see his old mistress.

'Ah, the road is so wet, and I forgot about my waterproof shoes,' he exclaimed when he was returning to his room.

'You needn't put on waterproof shoes, teacher, because some-one has already spread sawdust on the road,' a very nice boy said to the teacher.

'Well, then, I needn't trouble to put on my waterproof shoes.' So he started out again. Suddenly with a big splash he walked into a pool of water. As he was walking very rapidly, the dirty water splashed all over him.

'Who was the little devil who spread the sawdust on the ground? Come back, come back, all of you!' He was exceedingly angry, and was roaring and almost in tears. The students had to come back, and nobody knew who was the guilty person. It was a very funny sight to see the teacher with muddy water all over him. Soon the children saw the comic side of the matter, and began to giggle.

'Who did this? I must know who did this!' he shouted at us. None of the students knew who had done it. They looked at each other with suspicion, and I was the only one who had no doubt in my mind.

After he had examined everybody my turn came at last.

'Miss Phoenix, it must be you who did it. You are the naughtiest pupil in this school. None of the others would dare to do this.' He wiped his face and stared at me.

'You are joking, teacher. If the boys dare not do this, how

would I dare to do it? You said I was naughty, but you have no proof against me.' I made a very strong protest in order to make him realise that he had wronged me.

'When I was punishing Fu-Pan, I do not think you were here,' said the teacher. This must just have been his suspicion, for I do not think he really observed my absence. Nevertheless, I preferred to be discreet.

'No, I was not here, but I had a reason.' I tried to look very annoyed and stared at him.

'Tell me where you were.'

'No, I won't.'

'Then it was you! Or else you would say where you were.'

'I cannot tell you because it is not nice to say it.'

'Then I will punish you.'

I saw he was in earnest.

'Well, if you must know, I went to the lavatory.' And I pretended I was almost in tears.

All the students tried their best to suppress their laughter, and the teacher was more embarrassed than any one of us.

'All right, we will talk about that to-morrow.'

So we were at last dismissed.

On our way home we were all guessing who had done this. Most of them were very pleased with the result, but one of them said:

'But it was a shame, because his only garment was soiled.'

Another boy joined in: 'The garment doesn't matter very much. It is a real shame to keep his mistress waiting longer than she should.'

We all enjoyed the joke. But the unfortunate boy who had advised the teacher not to put on his waterproof shoes was severely scolded by the teacher the next day. Though it was plain that he did not do it, the teacher was angry with him.

Chapter VII

MY UNSUCCESSFUL ATTEMPT AT SUICIDE

DURING that winter a letter came from my eldest brother in Changsha to my mother, in which he said about me:

'My younger sister Phoenix is very talented and should be given a thorough education. Next spring I think it would be a good idea to send her to the Da Tung Girls' School for further studies, so as to lay the foundation for entrance to a girl teachers' school. During the past few years girls have been encouraged to come out of their corners and many girls' schools have been established. As our family is well known for its fragrant odour of books, I hope my kind mother will not keep my younger sister at home only because she is a girl.'

I was very grateful to my eldest brother. I really do not know why he was so good to me. My future was full of hope. I was so happy that I did not sleep at all that night, but was thinking of the time when I should go into Da Tung Girls' School. I would study very hard and hoped to read more books than my elder brothers had done. I kept on thinking about this.

At that time my father, my second elder brother and my third elder brother were all away from home. My elder sister had just had a baby and was very busy. She wanted to get a nurse for the baby but was not allowed to do so.

'I must go to the Da Tung Girls' School to study in the spring,' I said to my mother.

'What is the use of your studying any more? A girl who has read as many books as you already have done has done quite enough. You are not a man. What sort of use can you make of these books?'

My mother paid very little heed to what I said and gave me this disappointing reply.

'Has not my elder brother written to you asking you to send me to the Da Tung Girls' School?' I asked her in a very sweet voice.

'What does he know about this? A mother can take care of her daughter and does not want other people's advice. From next year you will have to start to do embroidery, and I must try to bind your feet a little bit smaller. If I marry you off as you are now people will say that I did not bring you up properly.'

'But Mother, I want to study, as my brothers have done. I don't want to do embroidery. Why won't you allow me to study like my brothers? Am I not a human being just like them?'

'Nonsense! What do you know about human beings? After boys have studied they can become Government officials. You are a girl who can only be a dutiful wife and a good mother, looking after your parents-in-law and the affairs of your family. What possible need is there for you to study?'

At that time I could not say why I should go and study, neither could I argue with my mother about the equality of boys and girls, and certainly I could not tell her that a girl, after having studied, could do a lot of good in the world. I only knew that I wanted to study. I wanted to acquire new knowledge, just as I liked to have my meals and clothes. I could not understand why a girl was bound to be nothing but a wife, to give birth to children for her husband and to be badly treated by her parents-in-law, just as was happening to my elder sister.

Tear-drops as big as green peas fell from my eyes and I was trembling all over. I never thought my mother could be so cruel to me. Her expression was so fierce that I dreaded to look at her.

'Above all, you are a very bad girl,' said my mother, with an angry look at me. 'You are worse than any of the boys, and are well known as the naughtiest student in your school. Severe as your teacher is, he cannot control you at all. If you go on studying you may break your way into the heavens!'

From henceforth I was not allowed to bring up the question of my studies any more. I knew my mother would never compromise, so the only way for me was to wait until the return of my father. Then perhaps there would be some hope. But my father was a very hen-pecked husband; to whatever his wife said he was obliged to consent. Therefore the question of my continuing my studies seemed indeed hopeless.

Spring came, and everything on the earth was breaking into new life again. But I was preparing to embark upon the road of death. At first both my father and my grandmother tried to put it very nicely to my mother that I should continue my schooling for another half year, but my mother flatly refused. Then my elder sister, my sister-in-law and my aunt also said nice things for me. Still she refused. When I realised that there was no further hope for me, I determined to commit suicide.

In our village, as far as I knew, there were only the following ways of committing suicide:

1. Hanging;
2. Drowning;
3. Swallowing matches;
4. Eating opium;
5. Swallowing a gold ring ; and
6. Cutting throat with a knife.

A child is always a child. Though he may determine to commit suicide, he is still afraid of pain. This may be comic, but it is a fact.

Each day when I was thinking of committing suicide I examined these different ways very carefully.

Now first, I remembered seeing a relative who died by hanging herself. Her tongue fell out and her expression was so horrible that I had to discard the idea immediately.

The second way was by throwing myself into the river. But realising that my stomach would be full of water and swollen as big as a drum, and that I would be picked out of the water by some man who would take off all my clothes in trying to get the water out of me, I decided not to do this. At that time I thought a girl's naked body must not be seen by any man.

The third way was the matches, which have a very repugnant smell to me.

The fourth way was also impracticable, because I could not get hold of any opium.

As for the fifth way, I had no gold ring, and to be truthful even if I had one I would not dare to swallow it because I could never forget the pain I had when I swallowed the piece of coin.

The sixth way was by throat-cutting. If the cut was not deep enough to end my life, the pain would be unbearable, and if they got a good surgeon to cure me it would be worse.

At last I determined to starve myself, and I stayed in my bed determined to die of hunger.

I stayed in bed two days and all the family thought that I was ill. My mother immediately sent for the doctor, who was no other than my teacher, and he said I had no disease at all.

When my elder sister saw that I was shedding tears and not eating anything she was greatly worried and constantly came to my bedside trying to comfort me.

'My good younger sister, what is the matter with you? If there is anything I can do for you I will.'

'Nobody could do anything for me!' My tears flowed incessantly.

'Tell me what it is.'

'I . . . I . . . want . . . to continue my studies.' When I had said these few words my elder sister also cried. She already had her own difficulties, and now she heard of mine she was heart-broken.

My mother must have known that all I wanted was to go on studying, so she would not look at me. This made me more determined than every to end my life.

'If my mother really loved her daughter, why should she not consent to allow me to study when she realised that I was going to die?'

I began to have doubts about my mother's love for me. But on the third day she yielded because she feared that I was really going to die. She made it a condition, however, that I must be a very good girl at home for two years before she would send me to school. During this period of preparation if I acted in the right way, then I should have my wish. Otherwise she would marry me off very soon.

With this slight ray of hope my life was saved.

Part Two

MY SCHOOLDAYS

Chapter VIII

MY FIRST SCHOOL

DURING these two years of preparation I tried my best to be a model girl. I hope I am not vain when I say that I was very successful in this. At least the result was very satisfactory, even to my mother, who was very difficult to please. When I was twelve, true to her promise, she sent me to the Da Tung Girls' School.

This is an elementary school, and quite different from my old private school in my own village. When I first crossed the threshold of the school and saw many lively girls playing with india-rubber balls, jumping, or playing at other games, I almost thought I had entered into Heaven. I was almost crazy with delight, and my heart was full of an unutterable happiness. Alas, though I was so happy spiritually, I suffered a severe drawback physically. My tightly bound feet would not allow me to do the things the other girls did. As part of the conditions my mother had imposed upon me had been that I was not to be allowed to go to school unless I had my feet tightly bound, what could I do? In this school, of course, there were many other little girls who were suffering in the same way as I was, and some very kind-hearted schoolmates, who were happily disposed in regard to their own feet, tried their best to persuade us to discard our bandages. I had consented to bind my feet only with the intention of getting into the school. Now that I was there, I began to think of going back on my promise. Very soon I began to feel that it was a great disgrace to have a pair of 'golden lilies,' so at last, in spite of misgivings, I gradually took away all the binding cloths, and my feet began to enjoy freedom. After I had done this I went out into the courtyard with bare feet one day when it was raining very hard. It was a very exciting sensation to let one's natural feet get into touch with the good earth—a pleasure which I had not known for many years.

In this school there were two teachers who came from Changsha. In this small country town those who had been to the capital of the province were regarded by us as having seen the world. From schoolmates I learned that both of them were widows. One of them was Mrs. Chiang, who was even more desolate because she had no children. They both treated us like their own children and we were very fond of them and called them 'Teacher Chiang' and 'Teacher Chow.' Indeed, they were more kind to us than our own mothers. They encouraged us to study more diligently, and told us not to bind our feet.

Our life here was very happy. Many of our schoolmates we felt were even dearer to us than sisters. If there was anything which we did not understand, the younger ones would ask the older ones and the new-comers would ask the old-timers to explain. After our classes we generally went to the Chung-Cha Mountain or to the San-Chi Bridge to play. We were indeed a group of happy little angels, playing and laughing all the time, knowing nothing of the troubles and sorrows of the world.

Then a little trouble suddenly started, breaking up this un-eventful and happy life. Mr. Chung, who taught us drawing, and Teacher Chiang, whom we loved so dearly before, were obliged to leave us. It happened like this. Mr. Chung was a young man with a disposition as gentle as a woman. When he was lecturing, or in conversation, he never spoke with a loud voice. A charming smile was always on his lips, and he liked to play with the children, considering all the students as his younger sisters. Therefore the students took a special liking to him, not regarding him as a formidable teacher but rather as a dear friend.

One day Teacher Chiang called us elder students to the class-room and warned us not to hold conversations with the male teachers, and said that in the classroom we must be more dignified and our eyes must not leave our text-books to glance left or right. She added:

'Mr. Chung is very young and likes to smile. It is not very convenient for us to have a teacher like that in a girls' school. You are all "yellow flower" girls (unmarried girls) and should be very strict and careful in heeding the rules of propriety. To have too advanced an idea will not do at all!'

This was a bombshell! We all thought that her words were most insulting. The whole school rose against her. Within three days the trouble was known all over the city, as if the sky had fallen and the earth quaked.

We were a group of innocent little children. We knew nothing of the evil there was in the world. On the following day after this lecture, the first lesson in the morning was on natural science with Mr. Chung as the teacher. We sat before him in a very dignified manner and not a sound could be heard in the classroom.

'Take out your books,' said Mr. Chung with his usual smile.

None of us said or did anything. He did not observe the change, and opened his own text-book.

'To what species does cabbage belong, and what kind of flower has it? Min Kon, you answer me.'

Min Kon was my school name, given to me by my father. Following my name of Phoenix, this new name means 'Singing on the Hill.'

I gave no answer.

'What, you do not know? Yun Sin, can you answer me?'

Yun Sin, following my lead, neither answered nor looked at him.

'What is the matter with you? Have you all become dumb?' he said puzzled, but still with his charming smile.

'Please, teacher,' said Ho Sin, our leader. We all admired the courage of this schoolmate of ours, and our eyes were upon her. 'It is not because we have become dumb, but we have a very good reason for not answering you.'

'What is that?' There was a change of colour in his face.

'It is a very long story,' said Ho Sin, 'but I can put it very briefly to you. Simply because Teacher Chiang does not allow us to speak with you, we dare not answer your questions for fear she will suspect us of conducting ourselves contrary to the rules of propriety. I hope you understand our difficulty.'

'All right, I will resign. I am not qualified to be your teacher.' His face was red with rage. He took his text-book and went away in great anger.

Teacher Chiang, pretending that she did not know what was the matter, came to ask us why Mr. Chung had left the classroom before the bell had rung.

'You had better go and ask him,' some of us answered her.

She had to go to Mr. Chung and ask him to come back to his class, but she added that it would be better if he could suppress his smiles because all his students were young girls, and it would not look nice if other people saw them smiling at each other.

'Not to smile! What has that to do with my teaching?' Mr. Chung was in a great temper. 'I was born with a smile, and I smile at anybody or anything. Even when I see a dog or a pig I cannot pull a long face. I smile at flowers and trees, birds and beasts. What harm is there in a smile? Do you consider a smile as dangerous as a poisonous snake or a fierce tiger?'

Mr. Chung handed in his resignation. All the students of the other classes joined us. They all said Mr. Chung was a very good teacher and we must have him back. The headmaster asked us to send two representatives from each class to see Mr. Chung and entreat him to come back. On the third day after this Mr. Chung did come back to the school. We thought he was coming back for good, but it was only for a farewell address.

'Oh, my schoolmates,' he said in a dignified voice, and he succeeded in suppressing his usual smile. His face was very pale and he looked very angry. The auditorium was packed, for all the students, even those who were not quite well, came to listen to him.

'I have come here to say a word of farewell. As I am too angry to say much, I will only give you this advice. We are now working under very difficult circumstances. I only hope that you will be very diligent in your studies, so that you may become very useful in future and will be able to reform the present society and do away with all bad influence. You are all intelligent persons, just the same as boys. Why should you suffer because of the old moral code? You came to the school hoping to improve your knowledge. But what can you learn if you have to be treated like this? If you are not allowed to speak freely to your teacher you have lost your freedom of speech. If you are not allowed to smile or converse, what can I say about it? I hope you will take this incident as a severe lesson to you. You must rise against the imposition of the old moral code upon you and struggle to obtain freedom.

'As for myself, because of the present circumstances I cannot stay here but am leaving to-morrow. Until fundamental changes take place here I am not coming back. Farewell, my students. I pray that you will have a bright future and that you will struggle on to obtain your freedom!'

When we heard that he was going, we all trembled. With tears in our eyes we saw him walk away, and soon he was gone. Alas, our kind, helpful Mr. Chung was no more with us. We, like the peaches and plums in the orchard, had suddenly lost the spring wind. We, like a group of gentle lambs, had suddenly lost our leader and were waiting at the cross-roads. We looked longingly here and there and we cried:

'Our dear teacher, when are you coming back to us?'

This little trouble did not end here. The boys' school heard of it and they also went on strike, asking the headmaster to get Mr. Chung back, as he was also their teacher for natural science and drawing. Of course, we girls were on strike already, and we demanded that the authorities should do something to restore our good name, which we considered had been damaged by Teacher Chiang's insinuations. A demand was made that unless Teacher Chiang was dismissed we would all go back to our homes.

This went on for some time, and at last Teacher Chiang, asking for sick leave, left us. We were not pleased with the outcome because she was not dismissed but went away of her own accord, and the school authorities were not pleased because they thought we were too rebellious.

After resuming our classes for two weeks, the school decided to have the examinations earlier, and as soon as they were finished we were sent home earlier than usual for the summer holiday.

Chapter IX

MORE SCHOOLS AND MORE TROUBLES

Autumn came, and the time for school arrived again.

When my mother saw that my tiny bound feet had become large, flat, ugly things she was very angry, and almost heartbroken. On the one hand she scolded me severely for not obeying her orders, and on the other hand she complained that the school authorities had not respected the instructions of the parents of the students. Naturally she thought it was a great disgrace to have a daughter with a pair of feet as big and flat as two palm-leaf fans, and it was all the more bitter for her because she had wasted all her trouble in past years in binding my feet to a pair of small 'golden lilies.'

She did not want to send me to school again, but I entreated her, and also my father. Luckily my school report was very good. I was the top student of the top class. But as my mother was not pleased with the authorities of the school, it was decided that my father was to take me to the county seat and to send me to the County Higher Elementary School for Girls.

As I was the only girl from the town of Da Tung at the county seat, I was quite at a loss in the new school. My country accent was different from that of the county seat school girls, and for the first month or two I had almost no friends. I saw the other girls talking and laughing together, but I could not mix with them at first. After our classes I generally went to my room to read. Besides reading the lessons of the day, I also liked to borrow books from the library to glance through them. There were the *Youth Magazine* and the periodical *Little Friends* which I liked very much. I also liked to read stories of adventure and detective novels.

One day I saw on the public notice-board a little slip with my name on it saying that there was a registered parcel for me. I went to the authorities immediately and claimed the parcel, and found it contained a pile of new books sent to me from the Province of Shansi by my second elder brother. Amongst them were two books which did me a lot of good; one was a collection of famous new speeches, and the other was a collection of short stories. I was so delighted with the arrival of this parcel that I approached several schoolmates and addressed to them this very foolish remark:

'My elder brother has sent me many books and on the parcel there were a lot of postage stamps. It came from the Province of Shansi!'

As I was not a very good speaker, I always stammered when I stood on a platform. I would tremble all over, while my face became blue and my lips white, and I would scarcely know what I was saying. This book of speeches would help me a great deal, and I hoped it would do me a lot of good later on.

On the very night of the arrival of the books I started to read the collection of short stories. They were translated by Dr. Hu Shih, and were extremely readable in spite of being translations. I finished half the book at one sitting, and I was deeply moved by two stories named 'The Last Lesson' and 'Two Fishermen.' To be honest, some of the stories were quite beyond me, and I could not possibly understand what they meant. I also liked the story of 'The Son who Killed his Parents.' It aroused great interest in me, and I admired the courage of the boy while at the same time hating his cruel mother. This made me begin to have a very good feeling towards the new style of writing. I read the book over and over, three or four times, without losing interest in it. It seemed to me that the more times one read it, the more interesting it became, and one could not bear to put it down.

At that time, if a student had written a good essay, drawn a good picture, done a piece of good handicraft or a piece of good handwriting, they would be posted in a public place for exhibition. My handwriting was awful, as it was always hurriedly done, and it never had been put on the wall or gained a good mark. Nevertheless, my little essays were often singled out for exhibition. My father specially bought me some very good models of calligraphy, the copy-books of Chao and the copy-books of Yen, for my benefit. He wanted me to choose one of them to copy, but I never practised either of them. One day when he received a letter from me the handwriting of which must have been particularly awful, he came across the river to scold me.

'Whose model are you following? Your handwriting is terrible!'

'I . . . I . . .'

'Whose model?' My father was angry.

'Min Kon's model.'

'What?' My father was puzzled by the strange calligraphist.

'I am not using any copy-books. I am following my own model.'

My father was amused, and laughed.

Very soon I was taken from this school to be sent to another. When I heard my mother had consented to send me to the city of Yi Yang to enter a better school, I could scarcely believe it until she herself told me.

'As your eldest brother is the headmaster of a school in Yi Yang, and your eldest sister-in-law would never consent to come back here, I thought I had better send you to that city so that you will have them to look after you.'

At that time I did not at all know how to thank my mother. I really felt that she was the most loving, the most considerate and the best mother in the world.

From my home to the city of Yi Yang was a journey of more than six hundred *li*. By travelling in a junk with a favourable wind it would take at least four days. It was really beyond my dreams that my mother should allow me to study in a college at such a distance.

Perhaps I was destined to be an exile, for I didn't feel the least regret or sorrow when I learned that I was to leave my home and live so far away. Though I could not refrain from shedding a few tears when I saw my mother and grandmother and elder sister crying at my departure, I was really happy and light-hearted when the boat set sail. When I was passing places where the landscape was pleasant, I forgot everything and enjoyed the scenes of nature in silence.

On the Saturday after my arrival at Yi Yang, my eldest brother sent me to the Shin Yi Girls' School (the Girls' School of Faith and Righteousness), which was run by an elderly lady from Norway whose name was Miss Ella. She was more than forty years old and still unmarried. This was the most comprehensive school in Yi Yang, for it had a primary elementary school, a higher elementary school, a middle school, a normal school and a college in it. It was well-equipped and well-staffed. There were more than two thousand students in it, and they were all living under the control of 'God.'

I am a 'barbarian.' From a very early age I mixed with boys, and I am not afraid of anybody, which of course includes 'foreign devils.' I never thought that in a Mission School there would be so strict an entrance examination. I had been in the first year of the Higher Elementary School, and naturally I thought I could be admitted to the second year in this school. But who would have thought that they would decide to put me in the first year once more? Perhaps my papers on English and Mathematics were not very good, as the questions were very difficult. For instance, in English I had only learnt to write very simple sentences, but in the examination paper here there were many questions on grammar. I knew nothing about passive or active voice, and I cannot remember what I wrote in answer to that question. As for Mathematics, I had not started fractions and proportion sums, and had to answer these questions with my own inventions. The result of this entrance examination, therefore, admitted me to the second term of the higher first year.

A girl from the country being suddenly transposed to live in a foreign mansion of four storeys seemed comparable to a beggar being suddenly made into an emperor, and perhaps my joy was even greater than that of the beggar. In this school one could not only be exempted from paying tuition and boarding fees, but a grant could also be made to the really poor student for pocket money. I came from a comparatively better-off family, so I had to pay ten silver dollars a term for boarding fees. Yes, this could be called a free and comfortable school, and we all seemed happy there. The buildings were large and lofty, very quiet, and with plenty of fresh air, with the River Tze running behind the school. It was an ideal place for education. Often, on hot summer days, we would feel intoxicated by enjoying the gentle cool breeze coming from the river. At sunset we would go up to the third storey and gather in groups of three or five to look at the distant sails on the river, with the beautiful background of the crimson and gold rays of the setting sun. Sometimes we could hear the entrancing songs of the fishermen, who came slowly in their light boats towards their homes. The gentle river breeze brought to us wave after wave of the fragrance of flowers. The white sails on the river looked as light as the wings of the seagulls coming and going. The distant mountains were generally wrapped in a thin layer of mist. This was indeed a picture full of poetical inspiration.

The most beautiful scene was that in the early morning of a summer day. The little birds would be twittering their morning songs on the branches. The weeping willows on the banks of the river would wave gracefully in the gentle wind. The ground was covered entirely with green grass, and the sun would creep up slowly from the east in the blue sky like a very shy girl emerging from her bath with a smile on her lips. By and by the sun's rays would reach the river, which very soon became bright red, and slowly all the mountains would turn red as well. Oh, I liked the bright red sun. It was dignified and majestic and shone all over the universe.

I loved the sun, and if it was not raining I generally got up very early by myself. Although sometimes I could not see the sunrise, I would not be disappointed. I liked to breathe the fresh air in the early morning. I also liked to do a little exercise with dumb-bells. I was very healthy and strong.

All my schoolmates were very kind to me and they liked to play with me. Also my teacher said I was clever, and although I refused to write an essay on 'The Sun Never Sets on the Union Jack,' and had expressed my disagreement with Imperialism, I was not scolded by the teacher. I was nicknamed by my schoolmates 'Princess of Happiness,' as I did not worry about my lessons, and I was smiling, playing and jumping all day long, as cheerful as a little sparrow.

But unknown to the others, since the day I had entered the school there was a kind of suppressed feeling in my heart. I did not believe in God, and never wanted to read the Bible, either the New Testament or the Old Testament. I hated to say before every meal 'Our Father in Heaven, hallowed be Thy Name, Thy Kingdom come . . .' I liked to sing, but I hated to sing the hymn 'God loves me boundlessly, and when I leave the world I will be saved.' Because I did not like to join in the prayers, I preferred to hide in such a miserable spot as the lavatory in the early morning and evening. Once I was caught by Miss Wu, whose charge was to look after the behaviour of the girls. She had discovered that I was always late coming in for meals.

'Why are you always a little bit later than the others in coming to meals?' she asked me.

'I am always reading, and seldom hear the ringing of the bell.'

'What do you read?'

'The Bible.'

'Really? But I thought you did not like the Bible.'

'Who said I did not like the Bible? Formerly I could not appreciate such a good book. Now I feel that God is the only saviour of the world. I must believe in Him and worship Him.'

' "Thou shalt not lie," and remember to come to prayers before every meal.' She smiled and stroked my head very gently.

'Of course,' I said aloud. And in my heart I said: 'Only God knows!'

At that time I was very ignorant and simple-minded. I had no deep and proven theory for my atheistic views. I only felt that God did not exist and that 'all those who believe in God will be saved' was ridiculous. I kept on asking myself, Why then was it that all these poor and wretched people who came every Sunday to the services were always so poor as to be needing their daily bread? Why couldn't the God in whom they believed give them clothing, food and shelter? Why couldn't He heal them of their diseases and find some work for them to do? I also hated the excuse that was given, that these people were sinful and that God was punishing them. This was a poor excuse. I held that man is the god who created the world. Everything depends upon ourselves and not upon God. I never believed there was such a person as God.

My atheistic views and my avoidance of the Sunday services were known to my eldest brother. He came to the school immediately to warn me.

'My younger sister, please stop being troublesome, otherwise you will be expelled from the school. If that happens all I can do will be to send you home and you will never be able to dream of going to school again.'

On that night I did not sleep at all. What should I do? I could not make myself believe in God. If I was expelled simply because I refused to be baptised I was resigned to my fate.

The 7th of May came, and that was the day of National Shame (the day on which Japan handed China the twenty-one demands regarding special rights in the Shantung Province). All the schools and public organisations were closed to enable people to join in the great demonstration. Our school received a notice two days before the occasion from the Students' Union requesting us to join the parade at eight o'clock in the morning of the 7th. Though the notice was made public, the school was not closed on that day and the classes went on.

'Why don't we close the school for the day?' I asked one of my schoolmates when I heard the morning bell.

'Why?' She really had forgotten what day it was.

'Don't you know it is the day of National Shame?'

'This school never joins in such things.'

'Are we not going to join the parade?'

'Of course not.'

'Why?'

'You must realise that Norway is also one of the imperialist countries. One of the slogans of the paraders is "Down with Imperialism!" Do you think the authorities would allow their students to shout "down with themselves"?'

'We must all go, no matter what happens,' I shouted.

'Yes, let us all go!'

I was joined by many schoolmates.

'We must ask the school authorities to close the school for the day and let us remember the day of our National Shame.'

We set out immediately to speak to students of other classes, and very soon the whole elementary school department joined us. Then the normal school department, seeing what we had done, became restless, and very soon the first, second and third year of that department decided to stop lessons. Only the fourth year, who were to graduate very soon, decided to shut the doors of the classroom and continue their lessons and their lectures.

Though we were not having our lessons, we were forbidden to go out and join the parade, and of course the school door was locked. I thought of continuing our struggle with the school authorities, but an older schoolmate said:

'What we have done this year is already record-breaking. I think we should stop here. If we go any further it is most probable that the ringleaders will be expelled immediately.'

'Then let us have a ceremony in the school.' I appealed to the students, and I had a majority.

While we heard the drums and bugles, and the shouting of the slogan 'Down with Imperialism' from outside, we also wanted to do something on the same lines. We wrote our slogans on pieces of paper torn from our exercise books and pasted them on chopsticks. We organised a parade going from the playground to the upstairs floors, and then from there to the ground again. While we were parading we, like the students in the streets, were equally excited and full of enthusiasm. We shouted loudly, 'Down with Imperialism!' 'We Want Freedom of Speech!' 'We Want to Join the Students' Union!' 'We must wipe away our National Shame!'

Unfortunately these slogans were recorded by Miss Tang, who was a spy for the headmistress. Immediately she reported us to 'Yellow Eyeballs,' which was our nickname for the headmistress; she was very angry, and we were summoned to the auditorium by the ringing of the bell. She lectured us for a long while and threatened that if this went on the ringleaders would be expelled immediately.

'What do I care!' If they want to expel me, let them do it. Do they think that we should have no regard for our country simply because of the fear of being expelled?' we said to each other. 'Of course we are not afraid of them.'

'Even if they killed us, it would not alter our patriotic feelings,' we added.

Our headmistress was not afraid of us either. Although she did not expel me publicly, she did not like to keep a disturbing element in her school. As a compromise, 'Yellow Eyeballs' summoned my eldest brother and asked him to take me home.

'Your sister is too naughty for my school. She is always acting against the school authorities, and especially this time she has created great disturbance. According to the regulations she must be expelled. But in consideration of you, sir, who are a well-known personality in the city, and also in consideration of your younger sister, who is a clever and altogether lovable girl, we do not want to spoil her future, and so we will not expel her publicly but ask you, sir, to take her home with you.'

That was a very polite speech. My eldest brother heard this as though it were a thunderbolt from a blue sky. As for myself, it was my destiny. On that very afternoon I had to leave the School of God. The result of my being patriotic was to be expelled.

CHAPTER X

HEADMASTER GRANDMA

As I have said, my mother had a very perverse temper, and as soon as she heard that I was expelled from the school, she immediately resolved that I should be sent to another school.

The next school I attended was the First Provincial Normal School for Girls in Changsha. It was established by the Provincial Government of Hunan, and none of the students had to pay any tuition or boarding fees, or for books and stationery. Two students were allowed from each county every year, but they had to pass a very stiff entrance examination. When my father took me to Changsha he was not at all sure whether I would be successful. As I was still a student just finishing the first year of the Higher Elementary School, I was really making a jump of two years' study in my attempt. Since this was a free school, there were many candidates at the examination, but very fortunately I passed.

When I entered the school I found that I had no trouble in following the Chinese History and Geography classes, but in Science I fell a long way behind the standard. I had to work very hard for two months before I made enough progress to be able to follow the other classes without difficulty. My schoolmates were all very kind to me, and soon became my friends. Our school life was very happy because we had a very good headmaster, who was none other than the scholarly Mr. Shu Te-Li, who also had advanced ideas. When I first entered the school the headmistress was a very delicate and beautiful lady who was a feminist, and not quite capable of looking after the school. As soon as she resigned we had Mr. Shu. He was a great educator. The moment he came to our school the atmosphere was entirely changed. We were no longer told to read nothing but dead books, but were taught to be useful citizens of the world. Because he loved us as much as if we were his own children, and because in appearance he looked rather like an elderly lady, we gave him the nickname of 'Grandma.' He was strict in some ways. For instance, he would

3 *   69

not allow us to wear very tight vests, as was fashionable at that time. He would not allow us to eat hot peppers and chili, which was a general habit among people of that district. He would not allow us to read after certain hours at night, and he would inspect the rooms every night to make sure that everyone was in bed. He said that as we were growing girls we must have a healthy body before we could have a healthy mind. At the time of examinations he would become a very formidable figure. He did not believe in cramming our brains in a short time, and he would look in every dark corner with a torch in order to get all the students to go to their dormitories to sleep. If he found any of us burning a candle to do our lessons after the electric light had been turned out at a certain hour, he would scold us severely.

In winter time the classrooms were heated when the days began to grow cold. He would ask every one of us whether we had sufficiently warm clothes. We must be careful not to catch cold. In the summer time he came to see that the windows were open and all the rooms properly ventilated. At that time there was a general tendency among the students to eat broad beans, as a child might eat sweets, at all times of the day. When the students were walking in small groups on the verandahs and in the playground of the school, each of them would have a handful of broad beans which they would be eating and spitting out the husks all over the place. Our Grandma did not scold us for this, but he stooped down and picked up all the husks he could find. When the students were enjoying their morsels, they were surprised and touched to find Grandma following them everywhere and picking up the litter behind them. He would say to them: 'Please do not throw them all over the place. My back aches when I stoop too much.'

This touching little act cured us of the very bad habit of leaving broad-bean husks and peanut shells all over the place. From henceforth even waste paper was rarely seen on the ground. We could not but admire him and his methods of education.

Once he learned that two of the students were of loose character. One of them did not return to school for the night, and though there was a note from her asking leave of absence for the night, our Grandma had found out where she was spending the time. On the following day he sent for her, and she at first said that she was kept at home. Our Grandma knew that the girl was frightened in case she would be expelled if she confessed, so he said very kindly to her:

'I went to your house last night, and I know where you were, but please understand that I am only trying to help you. You must tell me, confidentially, what made you spend the night at a hotel. Was it because of love, or are there other reasons which forced you to do so?'

Tears rolled down her cheeks. From her expression our Grandma knew she was a helpless girl. He comforted her with many kind words and assured her that she would never be expelled because of this. She then told him that because of financial difficulties, she was forced to do a thing which was repugnant to her. Our Grandma immediately promised to give her twenty silver dollars a month to help her out of her difficulties, and told her to pursue her studies diligently and never go out again.

He did the same thing with the other student, and these two girls, whose names I cannot divulge, became very good scholars. Their bad name among the students was entirely wiped clean and everybody respected them.

Because of helping poor students financially, and because of making donations to the library to buy new books, he was never able to send any money to his home. Neither did he care to spend anything on himself. He was generally dressed in an old worn long gown, and all his belongings were scarcely more than the old coverlet on his bed. In the spring of 1926, when the mutinied soldiers of a certain General Yeh came to besiege and attack the school, they took him to be the cook, and made a fierce attack on Mr. Shah, who was wearing a western suit. Poor Mr. Shah was severely beaten by the soldiers.

At the end of each term he would look carefully over the reports of the students. Whenever he saw a girl was not doing so well because she was not so young, he would tell her the story of how he himself studied.

'I went to France to study when I was already forty-seven years of age. I knew no French when I went there, and I was not sorry to start at such a late age. In my class most of the students were six or seven years old, for I had to start from A.B.C. Some of the children called me "Grandpapa" and liked to sit in my lap playing with my grey beard. I did not mind them at all. Of course my memory was not as good as theirs, but I knew how to study better than they did. Even if I just learned one word a day, I could learn three hundred and sixty-five words in a year. Never mind about your age. It only matters whether you study diligently or not.'

He was one of the very few who hold that boys and girls should have freedom of social intercourse. He would never inspect nor censor the students' letters. 'What is the use of censoring letters? You can only prohibit what is put down on paper; you cannot do anything with the mind. Young people are always young people. As long as they are not neglecting their studies, why should we not allow them to love each other?' This was what he once said to a mistress who strongly recommended the censoring of our letters. She thought his remarks were scandalous.

His daughter had a love affair with a young man, and it did not turn out to be a success. She then wrote a book entitled *Tragedy of Love*. At that time this was considered as a disgrace by old-fashioned people. They said that Mr. Shu would not have the face to meet his friends because he had a daughter who acted contrary to the rules of propriety. But he did not care about it at all. On the contrary, he said that his girl was a woman of spirit.

'My daughter is full of revolutionary ideas, and she would never allow circumstances to bind her as most of the old-fashioned girls had been bound by the obsolete laws of the dead. To fail in love is a very ordinary thing and nothing to be ashamed of. It is only through failure that you can be successful.' That was his candid remark.

CHAPTER XI

MY FIRST LITERARY ATTEMPT

OF course, at that time my ideas were also very advanced. I liked to read new books, study all kind of new theories, and mix with people from various literary associations.

Our school library was one of the best in the province. It was full of books written by people with new ideas, and the latest magazines and periodicals were plentiful. Our Grandma often said: 'I had rather give up eating my rice for a day than to stop reading for a day. For rice you can get anywhere and any day, while good books are rather difficult to find.'

I was in charge of the library, and two representatives were selected from each class to help me. When I was on duty in the library I would always have a book beside me, and could read as much as I liked when I was not busy checking the lending and returning of the books.

I liked novels, no matter whether they were new or old. No matter what they were about, I always wanted to scan them all over. Among the old novels I liked best *Shui Hu* (which Miss Pearl Buck has translated as *All Men are Brothers*). That most famous book, *The Dream of the Red Chamber*, did not arouse my interest. I hated Lin Tai-Yu sobbing all the time, and I hated all of Chia Pao-Yu's behaviour. He only knew how to play with girls and must be considered as an abnormal idiot. I had a great admiration for the heroes described in the Shui Hu. They are really heroes, and their spirit inspired me later on to join the Army.

The Student Movement of the 4th of May began in Peking, and it resulted in a course of new literature for China. I liked very much to read books published by the Creative Society and such authors as Kuo Mo-Jo, Yui Ta-Fu and Chen Fan-Wu. Among foreign authors I liked to read the works of Guy de Maupassant, Zola, Tolstoi and Dostoievsky. Miss Lu Yin and Miss Ping Hsin were the two foremost women authors of the period, but I did not like their work as well as I did that of Miss Pai Wei, which made a much deeper impression on me. Miss Pai Wei had suffered from the tyrannic code of the old-fashioned society, and her book, *Fighting Out from the Pagoda of Ghosts*, was full of the spirit of resistance. But at that time I was not very firm in my ideas, and my appreciation of literature was also many-sided. For instance, *Salome*, by Oscar Wilde, and *The Lone Swan*, by Monk Man Ju, also aroused my interest. As for that famous work, *Die Leiden des Jungen Werther* by Goethe, which was very popular at that time, I read it five times. Indeed, that book made a very deep impression on me.

Sometimes when I was too deeply immersed in my book I would not notice a schoolmate who was standing before me to borrow a book. When they started to tease me for my absent-mindedness, I would put away the book and apologise.

I began to write stories when I was in the second year of the school. At that time I was fifteen years old. One day I went into the home of a general to have lunch. He came from my own county. He had just bought a slave girl of thirteen years of age. To me the girl seemed the picture of misery. She was pale and very thin, of very small stature, much too small for her age, and I seemed to see marks of tears on her cheeks. Her big black eyes, which were very lovely, had a very appealing effect on me. Her new mistress was the wife of a big Army general, and she ordered the girl to walk forwards and backwards before us so that we could judge whether her gestures would be considered suitable for the services of a big house. My two schoolmates examined the poor girl carefully, but a fire was burning in my mind. I hated our hostess for her inhumanity. She was treating this poor girl like a domestic animal. I had scarcely any lunch at her house, and when I got home I immediately wrote an article entitled 'A Hurried Impression,' and signed it with a pen name. I sent it to the literary editor of *Ta Kung Pao* (a Chinese newspaper with the French title of *L'Impartial*), and a few days later I was filled with indescribable joy when I walked into the newspaper room at my school and found my article published in that paper.

That winter I was elected to be editor of the monthly magazine of the school. Of course this furnished me with a very good opportunity for writing. But I began to realise that my writing must be very childish and immature. I determined to read more books and acquire more new knowledge.

Talking about writing short stories, I remember a very amusing incident. Our classroom was very close to the city wall, and suddenly one day we found a lunatic walking to and fro on that part of the city wall, looking at us. He was clothed in rags and was murmuring all the time. Sometimes he would point his finger this way and that as if lecturing the people, and sometimes he would stop and cry aloud, while stamping his feet and shouting, 'Your mother! Your mother!' (bad language in China). We soon learned from someone who knew him that he had been a student in England, France, and Germany, and could also read Japanese and Russian. This linguistic scholar had gone crazy because of disappointment in love. The lady in question was from the Liu family, and so the lunatic often raised his voice and asked us:

'Is there a Miss Liu amongst you? I want Miss Liu, even if only just to see her for a short time!'

'No! Go away,' we often shouted back at him, but he would say to us in a very sorrowful tone:

'Have pity on me, please! Tell me where is Miss Liu? I must see her.' He shed tears and we were very sorry for him.

'Look, here comes Miss Liu,' once we teased him when one of our schoolmates of that name came to have a peep at him from our classroom.

'No, this is not the Miss Liu I am seeking.' Then he started to sob very bitterly, which made us all the more sorry for him, and we never dared to tease him again.

When he was in a happier mood he could be very amusing, and many of our schoolmates from other classes would come and crowd into our room to see the lunatic, and to hear him tell stories about England, France, America and Germany. Sometimes he would sing for us either comic or heroic songs, and he had a very good voice, but if we happened to say anything which was not to his liking he would tell us to go away, and if we refused to retire he would resort to an unpleasant action, which would have an infallible result, and that was to pull down his trousers. This was a more deadly blow to us than bombs or big guns. The moment we saw his hands on his trouser belt we would dash downstairs, sometimes rolling down in our haste. On several occasions he walked stark naked in torrents of rain, which made us never dare to look out of the window when we were in class having our lessons.

This lunatic gave us plenty of material for the school magazine, and also for our general conversation. Whenever a girl was in love we would say that she was on the way to creating one more lunatic in the world.

Chapter XII

PLATONIC LOVE

IT seemed very strange to me when I first perceived that many of my schoolmates began to become inseparable pairs. They would never leave each other, whether walking or sitting down, and that was something very new to me. There were quite a number of my old schoolmates in Changsha, and several of them were now studying in the same school with me. We were fairly good friends with each other, but there was no special attachment between any of us. But there was a Miss Sun, who also came from Shin-Fa and studied with me in the same class, and she suddenly fell in love with me. Indeed, she was a very unreasonable girl who could be described as full of flaming love. At first when I discovered that she was specially good to me I felt rather annoyed and thought she was tiresome. Every Saturday afternoon she would offer to accompany me to do any shopping I wanted to do, and if I happened to be staying in, neither would she leave the school on any account. She must stay in the same room with me. As the days went by, and perhaps because of her constancy, I, iron-hearted though I am, began to feel some affection for her. From my birth I had been quite like a boy, and she was a typical romantic girl.

Once, when I was very ill, she came to my bedside and watched over me for four days and three nights. She did not go to her lessons, neither did she go for her meals. All she had was some congee which was provided for the invalid. She went out to get medicine for me without getting permission from the school, and of course she was upbraided by the authorities for this. I was very grateful to her, for she was really the first woman I ever met who would sacrifice everything for her friend.

I really do not know what was the reason, but quite a number of my schoolmates liked me. To be quite frank, I had rather say they fell in love with me than to use the word 'liked.' Like Miss Sun, who doted on me, there were five others, and I really did not know what to do. There were two in the same class with me, and three from other classes. After our lessons they all wanted to keep me company, but I had to refuse them all, for I knew that I could only keep company with one of them at a time, and that would infuriate the others. Those from the other classes would say: 'You are from a different class from me. I am not really qualified to be your friend,' while those of my own class would say: 'I am not a literary genius, of course you will not keep me company.' Under such circumstances I was indeed in a great dilemma. Whenever any one of them asked me to play or enjoy some food with them, I always replied: 'Kindly excuse me just now, I am busy.' 'You are always busy,' was their reply, and while they were angry I had to smile back and try to forget it.

In the mornings after breakfast and before the classes, or in the evenings when twilight came, there were always numerous pairs of students walking and talking in the playground. But I always went in, to be alone by myself reading a book, or trying to find a remote corner where I could meditate.

'Why are you by yourself? Haven't you any friend?' our Grandma asked me with a broad smile, as if he knew what was my trouble.

'No, not because I have no friends, but because there are too many, which is even worse,' I replied with the same kind of smile.

'Dear child, I am sure you do not know how to deal with them!'

'I really do not know what to do. They are so jealous of each other. If they were not, we could be a big happy family together.'

But that was impossible. Once Miss Sun, finding me talking with a new friend, thought I was forgetting her devotion and taking on somebody else. She gave me an angry look and said:

'Did not you say that you were going to write some letters?'

'Yes, I have written those letters, but I want to do a little reading now.'

'Reading! You are doing it in a very strange way. Is your new friend the book?' And she went angrily away.

'Alas, what can I do?' I remarked to my new friend. She turned to go, and exclaimed:

'I am extremely sorry! I am not really your intimate friend, and have had the misfortune to create this jealousy.'

I really did not understand why they should be jealous of each other. In my own mind I thought that if A's friend could be

B's friend, and B could also be C's friend, and if one's friend could also be one's friend's friend, then we could all be friends, and it would be all right. But, alas, this was just one of my impracticable theories. None of them would share my views.

Sey and Su were two of my specially good friends. They were both gifted with literary talent, and their writings were very subtle, but they both had a rather tragic outlook on life, and their literary work was full of tragic atmosphere. I was of a different disposition; I was always optimistic. Whatever I wrote was full of joy and happiness. But I liked their writings very much, and thought my own work was too shallow and would not make a deep impression. In the same way, they liked my writing. They said that in being with me there was life, there was happiness, and there was a feeling of spring. Every Sunday we went out together, making trips to Yo-Lu Mountain, Sui-Lu Island, Shiang River or the Yui Garden. Besides these, there were many nameless forests where we often roamed.

At first my schoolmates did not notice our intimate friendship because I seldom went to their rooms and they never came to mine. Every time we went out, we always went separately and met in the house of my eldest brother. Later on our friendship became gradually known to some of them, and the news spread from one to ten and from ten to a hundred schoolmates. Of course, they exaggerated the matter very much, and they gave us the name of the 'Eternal Triangle.' Naturally we could do nothing about it. Miss Sun gradually became angry with me. She blamed me for not being constant to her, but I thought as I was not her lover, what was there to be constant about? Why couldn't we have two or more friends? I frankly told her that as she was so full of love she should place it on Miss Liao, who had a one-sided love for Miss Sun, and they could really make an ideal pair.

'No, I will not go away from you. I will love you always, and even if you do not respond to my love, I will still love you until death,' she said with resolution, and cried.

While I seemed unable to get myself out of one difficulty another trouble came upon me.

One day when I came back from my second elder brother's place, I found a letter on my bed not bearing a postage stamp. The writing on the envelope was delicate and had evidently been written by a girl. I opened it and read:

'To Min Kon, whom I adore and love, please excuse me for addressing you like this. This is a letter I have been wanting to write to you for a long time, but dared not. Now I cannot suppress my feelings any longer, and am presuming to write and send this letter to you. I shall deliver this letter to you while you are not in your room, because it would be very embarrassing to deliver it into your hands.

'Your writings I have read since the day I came to the school. What lovely essays they are! They make me intoxicated. From the first time I read your writings I felt I knew you personally, but, Min Kon, please forgive me a second time when I tell you that I have been following your shadow for a very long time. I always wanted to speak to you, to be near you, but would you care to make a friend of a very ignorant and childish girl? I am waiting anxiously for your answer. Your loving and doting friend, Kun.'

This was the first time I had received such a letter, and naturally I was more surprised than honoured. I knew this would not bring me any happiness, but would give me more trouble. I had to answer her very politely and humbly, and after that we became literary friends. We seldom talked together, but wrote a great deal to each other. Many of her writings were published in the school monthly magazine, and she was a girl of definite literary talent, and above all she was very intelligent. I liked her immensely but I did not like to speak with her, for which I felt very apologetic. She came from the county of Shiang Shiang, and she talked very much through her nose, which annoyed me a very great deal.

While sarcastic remarks about my having another literary friend began to circulate, a third important incident happened. There were in the 15th class two schoolmates who loved me. One was Miss San Shui Sha, whose love for me was really one-sided, for she composed many poems for me, and burnt them all. If it had not been for her classmate, Miss Li, who saw her strange doings, coming to tell me about them I would never have known anything about it. The other girl was a Miss Chen, whose love for me was even greater than that of Miss San. Besides writing love poems for me in her composition book, she told all her friends how much she loved me, and of course this became a popular subject with all her classmates. One day in the evening I was kidnapped as if by a band of bandits. They took hold of me and dragged me to Miss Chen's room.

Really, I never dreamt that such things could happen, but it seemed that this was quite a common happening among them. Very often after the school bell had sounded, a group of girls would gather to do some mischief, but I never thought that this would happen to me.

'What are you doing?' I asked them, surprised.

'We are inviting you to meet a friend,' someone who was not known to me answered.

'We invite you to sleep here to-night,' someone else said.

They all looked at me and also at Miss Chen, who did not dare to raise her head, and was blushing all over like a bride might do on the first night of marriage.

'This is not my room. How can I sleep here?' I said in a rude manner.

'This is as good as your room.'

'What nonsense are you talking!'

'Because Miss Chen's bed is as good as your bed, aha!'

They snatched away my shoes and pushed me into the bed. Good heavens!

'Look how much Miss Chen is in love with you. She has been following you for ages.'

'Why should Miss Chen love me so much? I don't even know her!' I was not afraid to offend Miss Chen's feelings.

'But she has known you for a long time, and has fallen in love with you and been dreaming about you many, many times,' and there was general laughter.

'The devils!' That was the first sentence Miss Chen had spoken. Evidently she was very angry too.

'Don't be angry. We will all go out and let you two have a lovers' talk.'

They went out immediately and bolted the door from the outside.

What was to be done? The only way I could get out seemed to be from the window, and it was too high to jump from.

I sat on the bed sullenly and felt miserable. There were other students sleeping in the same room, and I could distinctly hear their giggles coming from the three other beds.

'Go on and reveal your love for each other. Go ahead, Miss Chen, we will not listen to you.' This came from one of the beds.

'You can go on talking nonsense. I have nothing to say.' Miss Chen went to bed.

I felt I was sleeping in a tiger's den. I dare not move or speak.

As I could not possibly jump from the window I had to remain for the night in a stranger's bed. I was unable to sleep, and the next morning there would be an examination in biology. When I thought of this, I wished I could jump from the window. But I had no shoes. It was quite impossible for me to get away.

I sighed and sighed again, and heard the sound of all the watches of the night. Good heavens! it was the longest night I had ever known. I do not think Miss Chen had any sleep that night either. We kept a respectful distance from each other, and never a word passed between us.

I could imagine that she was full of tears, and I thought I could hear a suppressed sob. As she had such a great love for me and was so devoted to me, while I was so cold to her, not even giving her a word, this could be regarded as a great insult to her. But what could I do? I hate the habit of dragging people to meet unknown friends. I began to imagine the unhappy time a husband and wife must have who have no love for each other. Alas, they would just be as miserable as we were then. I was regarding Miss Chen as my enemy. I was afraid of her and angry with her. If this had not happened, and she had approached me nicely, we might have become friends. But after I had been dragged here by these mischievous people all was ended. There was no hope of our knowing each other. I wished I could say something to her, but could not find suitable words. It was raining outside all the night, and the trickle of the rain made me more uncomfortable in this strange bed. I knew she must also be having a very bad night, but I could not find a word to comfort her. At long last the morning bell sounded at six o'clock, and somebody unlocked the door and gave me my shoes.

'You must have had a very good night talking to each other about love.'

'Thank you for depriving me of a good night's rest!' I replied gruffly, and I was off like a whiff of smoke.

From henceforth I dare not go near this room. Even when I had to pass it on my way, I would rather take a longer route and go around it. In the playground or in the dining-room whenever I met Miss Chen I would drop my head and not look at her, while she would also try to avoid me as an old-fashioned girl would avoid meeting her fiancé. I, too, felt embarrassed.

CHAPTER XIII

A PUBLIC LOVE LETTER

CHANGSHA is a place with advanced ideas. From time to time, after the 4th of May movement, love affairs crept into every school in the city. But in girls' schools old-fashioned ideas still prevailed. Whenever a girl was in love with a man, no matter how ardently she felt for him, nothing would induce her to make any outward sign, and of course nobody would be daring enough to pursue a man. But with the boys it was different. Even if they had never met you, as soon as they knew your name they would write love letters to you. No matter whether you accepted their love or not, they would continue to write with a courage and persistence which would otherwise have been admirable.

The girls who generally received these love letters were either good athletes or those who made literary contributions to the papers, or else executives of the student associations. Every time that we had an athletic meeting large numbers of love letters, in pink or light green envelopes, would be delivered to our school by the postman. Those girls who played tennis, and our 'college basket-ball team members liked to display their letters and would say in a very charming way: 'Please look, I don't know what rascal has dared to write to me!'

I also twice unexpectedly received such letters. The first time was in 1924, after the spring-time athletic meeting. Not that I was an athlete, but I was the editor of the special athletic meeting number of our school magazine, and had made several contributions to fill up the space. Also I was a member of a group dance, in which I performed very badly. Because of these reasons, I received a letter from somebody, who said:

'Your body is as light as that of a butterfly and you dance as though you were a fairy. Your talent is as great as that of Tao Yun, and your knowledge is extensive enough to load five carriages.'

The second time was after I had been playing the part of a maid-servant in a performance of a play called *Whose Mistake is*

This? in the New Year's Union Meeting. I had a letter the next day from somebody who said that I was the best actress in the whole performance, that I was lovely as well as comic, that the way I delivered my speeches was brilliant, and that my movements were graceful. In reality that was the first time I had appeared on the stage, and because of lack of time for rehearsals I had given a very bad performance. That very exaggerated description of me made me shudder. I did not pay much attention to these letters; as soon as I received them I read them and then tore them up and threw them away. But there were some girls who took them very seriously and, wishing to get some publicity out of them, presented the letters to the school authorities. Sometimes they felt greatly insulted by them and cried bitterly.

The most ridiculous incident was the comedy of Miss Chen. On the day when we began our summer examinations I got up very early to prepare my English lesson when, as I was passing the public notice-board, I saw several pieces of pink note-paper with minute writing in blue ink. Curiosity drove me near it, and I observed that it was a love letter.

'My dear Miss Wong, Since your departure from Shanghai I have been thinking of you bitterly, as if I were living in a sea of misery. I hate the flowing water which carried you away and I hate the boat which severed me from you. Should you, like the falling flowers, have kind regards for me, let us pray that we shall become lovers in the next existence. If we love each other in our hearts nothing can separate us in spirit. While mountains and rivers may change their form and course, my love will never alter. I am a wounded person, and dare not have any further ventures with ladies, but you are a fairy among mortals. If I do not love you, whom do I love? If I could only hope that we could become literary friends and that we could express our love by pen and ink, then our meeting has not been too late, and we would be united in our coming lives. I do hope that you will not laugh at me, saying I am a fool, and perhaps will even condescend to write to me. When I look at the river and the sky I imagine that I can see you; my thoughts are full of you, and when I am writing to you I feel my spirit is by your side. Please forgive me for this letter, and if a fair wind blows this way, do let it bring a letter from you with it. Wu-Ting bows again and again.'

Strange to relate, I cannot understand what made me read this letter over and over again. Indeed, I read it aloud, like an old school teacher humming the *Book of Mencius* or the *Book of Confucius*. This induced many schoolmates to gather round me, and soon their number increased. They all followed suit, and soon a very big crowd was reading this letter in a roaring voice. Many people who would not have come this way joined in, and the crowd continued to grow until the second bell rang.

After this love letter had been read by all, many people were disturbed by it, and the following questions were brought up: (1) Why should a girl have this letter posted in public? Was it done by the receiver of the letter or by the school authorities? (2) Who was really the receiver of the letter? These questions continued to be asked by all of us, and not until the teacher came did we become quiet again.

'Be calm and quiet and answer these questions carefully,' said our teacher very loudly.

'Please teacher, it would be a good idea to ask us to write the love letter from memory. I am sure we would all get full marks,' I said then, and the whole class roared with laughter.

It was said that the writer of this letter was the husband of Miss Wong's intimate friend. Miss Wong went from Shanghai to Hangchou to visit various schools during her last year in the normal school, and on her return she received this letter. But the reason why she had the letter posted up in public was probably to indicate that she was a very pure and chaste woman and did not like to mix with men, and also to show her faithfulness to her friend. Really she could have torn the letter after she had received it. Why should she make a public show of it? She must have been a very queer woman.

As we could all recite this love letter, of course we added many of its phrases to our general conversation. Whenever the occasion arose, we would say: 'Should you, like the falling flowers, have kind regards for me,' or 'I do hope that you will not laugh at me, saying I am a fool, and perhaps will even condescend to write to me.'

CHAPTER XIV

THE BEGINNING OF MY STRUGGLES

WE had three different teachers for our Chinese lessons, and all
were very good teachers.

'We have now engaged the famous Mr. Li to take over the
Chinese classes, and I hope you will pay special attention to
literature. I presume you know that Mr. Li is the famous translator
of the works of Guy de Maupassant.'

After our headmaster's introduction we gave our new teacher
a hearty welcome.

We were very grateful to our headmaster because since our
school had been divided into two departments, one for Arts and
the other for Science, special attention had been paid to getting
a very good teacher for Chinese for the school of Arts. Although
our previous teachers for Chinese had always been good, the new
teacher, Mr. Li, inspired our respect and enthusiasm for literature
much more than anyone before him. We were all very happy, and
eagerly hoped that Mr. Li would give us good instruction. Even
some of us who hadn't paid much attention to literature thought
now that they would have a chance to go deeper into the subject. I
was particularly happy, because I always presumed that I should
prepare myself to become a novelist, and I was sure that Mr. Li
would not only polish my writing but also teach me how to be
more subtle in my descriptions. He would explain to me about the
planning, the construction, the technique and the polishing of a
piece of work.

So, on the first occasion when we were asked to write a composition for him, I wrote a novelette of about 10,000 words
entitled 'The First Love,' and was greatly hoping to see his
corrections. Who would have thought that two months would go
by and my composition would still be resting in one of his drawers?
In fact, that little work is still with him, and I have never seen it
since. I asked him several times about it, and he said he had not
the time to look over it. Later on I learned that, being a very able
man, he was the teacher for Chinese in four different schools, and

therefore spent much of his time every day driving about in his private rickshaw from one school to another, and when he arrived at his home he liked to enjoy the happiness of his family by fondling his numerous children on his knees. Then he had to do his own translation work, and consequently had not time to correct my wretched composition.

'Mr. Li, how about my composition?' I asked him every time he came to the school.

'I am really sorry, but I have no time,' he would answer very politely and also very formally.

'Then I need not write any further compositions for you?'

'If it is a very short one, not more than a few hundred words, of course I will do my best. Otherwise, forgive me for not having time.'

'What can I do? I cannot stop when I start writing.'

'Quality not quantity is what you want.'

'How can one acquire quality if one has no practice?'

'It will come to you gradually. You can polish your own writings, and gradually you will acquire quality.'

I was very much disappointed and said to myself: 'Why cannot I meet with somebody like Flaubert, who could teach me painstakingly? If I do not possess the talent of Guy de Maupassant, still I think I am a very earnest student and am doing my very best.'

Nor was Mr. Li a very good lecturer. Once he explained to us an essay by Flaubert, and as we were very eager to hear him, we were greatly disappointed to find the subject dry. It seems that some people who are very good writers and translators are not very good at teaching and lecturing. Besides, as he was so busy, I think he could not pay much attention to a group of young girls.

At the end of the term, after our examinations, a friend came rushing to me to tell me some unexpected news.

'Why, Min Kon, the mark on your composition was zero.'

'Have you seen the marks?'

'Yes, I noticed the big mark of zero on the sheet. The list has been posted on the notice-board.'

'That is absurd! Why should I get a zero mark? As I did write an essay, I should at least get some marks.' I was annoyed and also very ashamed. The mark of zero is not very complimentary.

'There is another thing which you must know, and probably it will make you more angry,' said my friend after a pause.

'I warn you that if all my marks are zeros, I did not come here to get marks but to acquire knowledge.'

'The essay which you wrote for Miss Wong in fifty minutes, and which you know was the only composition she handed in, acquired 85 points for her.'

'Ah, that is very good indeed. I am not angry at all. On the contrary, I am very pleased. I have really acquired 85 marks, and I don't mind having a zero in addition.'

There was another inducement which made me turn away from my studies. That was the 30th of May Massacre, when Chinese demonstrators along the Nanking Road in Shanghai were fired on and killed by British and Japanese policemen and marines. On the following day all the students in Changsha gave a big demonstration and paraded to the Provincial Government building, demanding that the authorities should probe into the matter, and also to tackle imperialist Japan so as to refuse her twenty-one demands. We wanted the dead to be avenged, and that their dependents should be looked after. When we were loudly shouting our slogan 'Down with Imperialism!' outside the Government building, we were suddenly informed that our representatives who went in to see the Governor of the Province had already been imprisoned. We demanded that they should be released, and as we waited but did not see our representatives again, the crowd tried to rush into the building, and more than a hundred students were arrested.

The provincial prison was very overcrowded, and many of the prisoners were confined in the offices of the jailors. Very soon the courtyard of the jail was used as a temporary place of confinement, and more troops and policemen were coming. But the mob was not intimidated and continued to rush forward. The secretary of the Governor's office saw that was not the proper way to deal with the students, so he stood on a high place and shouted to us:

'Because our Governor wanted to discuss the matter in detail with your representatives they have been detained for the time being. As it is impossible for the Governor to talk with all of you, I request all those who are not representatives to go home as soon as possible. This is a crisis of great importance for our country, and of course we will be responsible. You students should confine your attention to your studies.'

'Release all our schoolmates who have been arrested!' we shouted, and proclaimed that unless this was done we would not go home. This demand had its effect, and the secretary found that he could do nothing else but release all the arrested students, who numbered more than two hundred.

We went home at about nine o'clock in the evening, but we soon found out that all our representatives were still in prison.

On the following morning we organised many publicity groups to speak in public places. All day long we spoke to groups of people in the streets, telling them of the cruelty of the Imperialists and urging them to rise in resistance. All our listeners were greatly moved, and we noticed that our speeches had very good reactions.

The massacre of the 30th of May made us all realise what was our urgent need. All those hot-blooded youths, boys and girls, who had hitherto spent most of their time in the library, now realised that there was something else for them to do. They also awakened me to realise the fool I was. I knew nothing but to read over and over again *Die Leiden des Jungen Werther*. Alas, it was really dangerous. Had it not been for the second warning from the big guns of 1926 I might have become a second 'Jungen Werther.'

CHAPTER XV

MY FIRST LOVE

Extracts from my diary for 1926

LOVE THOUGHTS.

'I am really giving myself trouble. Why should his image appear in my mind? All I can see with my eyes is his smile, all I can hear with my ears is his voice. When I receive a letter from anybody I think it may be his, and I look at it over and over again to find out if I am right. My whole heart is occupied by him. Alas, what is to be done? I do not want to do anything. Whether in class or in the dining-room, or when I am waking or sleeping, I am always thinking of him. The lectures I cannot hear at all, and of my books I cannot understand a single word. In short, apart from sitting quietly and thinking of him, I simply do not exist.'

THINKING ALOUD.

'Honestly, I do not know what "love" is. What is it composed of? I have never tasted any love except a parent's love. I do not know whether it tastes bitter or sweet, sour or hot. All I know is that there is something mysterious about my feelings towards him. Can this really be called love?

'When I first met him, in the short twinkling of an eye when my eyes met his, the seed of love was sown in my heart, and it was like a piece of iron attracted by a magnet that my heart and soul went out to him. That was the first time in my life that I had had any kind of feeling for a person of the opposite sex. Whenever my schoolmates had talked about the question of love, I had always said "Pooh!" and then run away.

'They all said that I was an ignorant baby. I did not take offence, and I hoped that I would always be ignorant. But now an indescribable sorrow has suddenly come upon me. Oh, my heavens, what is this all about!

'I cannot understand the psychology of it. I love him, but I would never let him know it. I want to keep it a secret for ever and ever until the end of the world. Not to tell the one you love that you love him is a mysterious feeling which cannot be explained by the principles of psychology. Sorrow, sorrow, I welcome you! I will not avoid sorrow. Human beings are meant to suffer. Without sorrow, life would be meaningless. A certain author once said: "When you are in love, sorrow and tears are of value. When you are happily married, then you have entered the grave of love."

'The devil! why am I always thinking of this quotation? A pure innocent girl should not have such kind of things in her mind. . . .

'When for the first time in my life the image of a person of the opposite sex rushed into my mind, it made me feel so sorrowful that I wanted to commit suicide. I cannot understand why that image of the smiling young man is always before my eyes, making it impossible for me to read, or to pass my days without worry. I hate him, and I also hate my elder brother for introducing me to him. I wanted to destroy this image before me, but it was utterly impossible. Very often I wakened in the middle of the night because of a terrible dream, and then I would put my hand to my heart and scold myself severely.

'You worthless creature, you had better die. A pure and honourable young girl's mind should not preserve the image of a person of the opposite sex. That is a very unfortunate thing. Your future will be swept away by that image, like a dried leaf swept away by the wind. Your life will be destroyed by that image as a weak animal is destroyed by a beast of prey. This is very dangerous indeed. Extensive is the sea of sorrow, but the moment you turn back you will find that the shore of joy is near you. If you do not turn back quickly your life will be entirely ruined.

'No matter how hard I try to overcome my sentiments by my reason, my sentiments will always get the upper hand of my reason. Not only will that image not diminish, but it will become more lively and more active, jumping and dancing about before me every day.'

*   *   *   *   *   *   *   *   *

In such unhappy circumstances, I tried my best not to let anything be known by him. I had been in correspondence with him for over a year and never once hinted that I loved him and was thinking of him. I put my feelings in my diary and in my poems, and occasionally I would try to bury my thoughts in a cup of wine. Sometimes I would try to get some school friends to accompany me on a retreat into some very old temple to live in retirement, but nobody would follow me. Now I look back to those early days of my first love I think they were not altogether silly but were the bravest period of my life. The warning bell of the time had been sounded. The great Revolution of 1926 had broken out. Brave young men and young women had discarded their books and doffed their long coats and gone to join the Revolution. I, too, had been drawn into the sea of sorrow at that time.

That adorable image suddenly appeared before me in reality one day. This was the real image, the very person who came to me, and I felt his eyes looking at me with deep feeling.

'I am so glad you have come. I want to talk to you and have not time to write to you,' I said tenderly, for I was full of joy.

'What is it?'

'Would you believe it, I am going to join the Army!' Although I said it with a smile there was dignity in my voice. He began to look alarmed.

'I cannot believe it. You are only joking.'

'No, I am in earnest.'

'You cannot suffer the hardships of such a life.'

'I want to train myself for it.'

'Have you such determination?' Instead of his usual smile he looked sorrowful.

'I have already sent in my name as a candidate.'

'Think it over very carefully first. I hope to have a long talk with you before you decide.'

'No more thinking is needed. You should support my resolution unconditionally.'

'. . .' He looked down on the ground in silence, and I knew that his heart was full of indescribable sorrow. But strangely enough I did not feel sorry for him. Rather like a condemned person I felt I was suddenly reprieved, and I smiled very brightly at him.

'I am going back to-morrow. Tell me, can we meet again?' Somehow or other his voice was rather tragic and moved my heart. I began to feel lonely, but I was determined.

'We will meet at the front. I hope you will join the Army too.'

'. . .' His wordless reply came to me when I perceived that his eyes were glistening with tears.

Well, well, that was the last time I saw him. I said nothing and accompanied him to the gate of the school, and watched him with my eyes full of tears to see the image of him gradually disappear.

Part Three

MY ARMY LIFE

Chapter XVI

JOINING THE ARMY

I SHALL be grateful to my second elder brother until my death. It can be said that it was almost entirely because of him that I was able to join the Army.

During the summer vacation of 1926 I accompanied him to the Tao Shon Temple of the Yo Lu Mountain for his convalescence from consumption. At that time my mind was still deeply impressed with the image of the smiling young man, and I was downhearted and sometimes silent for a whole day. All I read was such books as *The Pavilion of Peony*, *The Notepaper of the Swallows*, *The Romance of the Western Chamber* and *The Love Story of the Lute*. My second elder brother was very angry with me, and one day he wrote a very long letter telling my father about me, and also scolded me severely. These words of his still linger in my memory:

'You woman, what a worthless creature you are! The bloody bell of the time has been sounded, and you are still snoring loudly in your dreams. Such stories of handsome young men and beautiful maidens should have been thrown away long ago, there is no meaning in them. The one is just like the other. You are an awakened woman and you used to like the new literature. Why don't you read some revolutionary works?'

He gave me *The A.B.C. of Communism*, *An Elementary Treatise on Socialism*, and some other introductory works to revolution. I immediately became interested in these books, and the image in my mind began to fade away gradually. The object of my writings also began to shift in the opposite direction. As I saw the life of many of the working people in the country, I began to describe their life and their sufferings, and these works were all published in the popular *Daily News* edited by my third elder brother. On the night before I sent in my name as a candidate for the Military School, I and my third elder brother went into my second elder brother's room in the Min Teh School to discuss whether I could be a good soldier.

'I opposed her going to join the Army. The life in the Army is dry, mechanical and hard. All day long the soldiers spend their time in "Attention," "At ease" and so on. Absolute obedience is their duty. Their brains are rusted through lack of use. To join the Army is not suitable for a person with literary talent, and on top of that I do not think her health would allow her to suffer the hardships.' That was what my third elder brother said.

'Your observations are all wrong. If she wants to create powerful and colourful works, in short, masterpieces, she must undergo some extraordinary life. To join the Army is to train her body, to nourish her mind and to furnish material for her writing. In short, it would give her every advantage and no disadvantage.'

Of course my second elder brother's views were entirely right, and my third elder brother had to give up his opposition, and we had no quarrel about it. As for myself, there is no need to say that even if they had both opposed my going, I would still have joined. Besides, my mother would force me to marry during the coming winter, and in order to get out of this difficulty I must leave the city of Changsha. But where could I go, a girl under twenty years of age and without half a piece of cash to bless herself with? Where could I go with a heart that was already wounded in youth? On this point I had the special sympathy of my second elder brother, as he himself was suffering from a marriage arranged by others, so he tried his best to get me into the Army. He said:

'This is the only way to free yourself. To join in the Revolution will enable you to solve all the other problems of marriage and the future.'

I believe that all the girl students who wanted to join the Army had as their motive, in nine cases out of ten, to get away from their families, by whom they were suppressed. They all wanted to find their own way out. But the moment they put on their uniform and shouldered their guns, their ideas became less selfish. By that time a girl began to think of the 1,250,000,000 oppressed people, the responsibility for whom she was taking on her shoulders. Most of our schoolmates who enlisted did so unknown to their families but not unknown to the school—for our headmaster, Mr. Shu, was the only person who was in favour of our joining the

4

Army. All the other schools forbade their girl students to enlist, so they secretly went to enlist as candidates for the Military School. Those who passed the examination were happy and overjoyed, and it is impossible to describe their cheerfulness in words. I still remember very clearly how, on an afternoon when it was pouring in torrents, 250 brave young soldiers, both male and female, gathered in the East Station at Changsha waiting for the train to carry them away. Many elderly ladies and young girls came to bid us farewell, and they secretly wiped away their tears with their handkerchiefs. But we were not sorry, at least I myself was not. I said:

'You people mustn't cry. You should encourage us to go and kill our enemies.'

Just then a young man unexpectedly came running towards me in the pouring rain and, panting for breath, handed me a pink envelope. He was the editor of *Flame*, a man utterly unknown to me. I was very sorry for him because I had no time to read the letter, and it was put aside for a very long time. Since I had decided to discard that image from my mind, anybody who came to offer me his warm feelings only received a douche of cold water.

We, the fifty girl soldier students, were all crowded into one car, and there was no room to sit down. We were rather like refugees, taking our small suitcases and bundles of clothes with us. This car had originally been meant for goods, so but for two iron doors there was not even a small window, and as we were miserable in the dark we began to sing loudly:

'Arise, ye starvelings, from your slumbers,
Arise, ye criminals of want!'

The moment we began to sing we felt happier, and we thought that we could really congratulate ourselves on the beginning of our new life and on our bright future. Every one of us was crazy, intoxicated, singing and jumping about.

CHAPTER XVII

COUNTRY GIRLS AND THE TRAIN

ABOUT five o'clock in the afternoon the train stopped at a certain station. I and Shu Yun hurriedly jumped out of the train and ran to a country house opposite the station. Many people looked at us with surprise in their eyes, but they did not stop us nor ask us the reason. It was inexcusably stupid and lacking in common sense that though it was our first trip by train we neglected to ask a vital question. We had the courage to become soldiers, could we not have had the courage to ask whether there was a lavatory on the train? We were the biggest fools in the world!

When we came out from the little house, only about two hundred yards from the station, we could not see our train any more. We were greatly alarmed, and like two mad dogs we started to run in the direction the train had gone. Four eyes looked ahead and four feet ran along, sometimes knocking against the iron rails and sometimes stumbling over the stones. Shu Yun was short and fat, so she often tumbled over, got up and then fell down again, rolling ahead rather than running along. Poor creatures, could there be more stupid people than we in the world, who were trying to overtake the train?

'We cannot overtake it. Let us turn back,' I said with disappointment. I did not know how far we had gone, but as we turned back we could not see the station any more. There were trees on both sides of us. Darkness began to descend. There were no houses and no travellers to be seen, and we began to tremble with fear. We started immediately to run back to where we had come from.

Our hearts were full of regret and disappointment.

'Stupid pigs! We're just a pair of stupid pigs,' Shu Yun said, almost with tears in her eyes.

'I am a country girl who has never been on a train before. But you come from Li Ling, which is served by a train. Don't you know how long the train stops at each station and where we could have found the lavatory?' I demanded of her, which made her more sorry than before.

'The devil! You are a country girl, so am I. What more do I know about the train than you?'

Down-hearted, we went into the house which we had not long since left with numerous 'Thank you's!' on our lips. A middle-aged woman asked us sarcastically:

'The train has gone. I wonder what you are going to do?'

'We will wait for the next train.'

'Don't wait here. Go and wait at the station.'

At that time we were very grateful to her, and as we were like two lost children in the woods, we were happy that suddenly somebody had come to give us advice. Therefore we went immediately to a place near the iron rails where we had got down.

We sat there waiting, waiting and waiting! One hour, two hours, three hours passed away, but there was no sign of the train coming from Changsha. The country was already wrapped in darkness, and we began to tremble with fear. Where were we going to spend the night? Where could we go to sleep? We were two girls from the country, without money and without luggage. Who would take us? We thought of kidnappers and were worrying ourselves to death. When we thought of kidnappers it seemed as if big, terrible shapes were moving towards us, with huge arms stretched out to get us. I said to my friend in a trembling voice:

'Shu Yun, let us go immediately to find some place to sleep. Staying here waiting for the train is too dangerous.'

We held each other's hands very tightly and crept in the dark to find our way to the nearest village.

'Madam, please will you open the door?' Through the crevice of the door we could see lamplight. We knocked on the door lightly and heard people speaking inside.

'Who is that?' It was a cold and fierce voice, and our courage left us. Our legs began to give way and we felt we could not stand erect.

'Let us try at another house,' Shu said softly to me.

'Madam, please have pity on us and open your door.'

'Go away. We do not give anything to beggars.' That was the voice of an elderly lady, and it was gentle.

'Elderly madam, we are not beggars. We are two girl students who have just lost their train. Please open your door and let us come in.'

Though we were not beggars, our plight was much worse than that of a beggar.

'At such a time of night how can there be good girls outside? I won't open the door.'

Good heavens! We were taken for some horrible creatures. Nobody would take us in. Where were we going to spend the night? A man's voice reached us; it did not sound very good.

'I welcome you!'

We felt as if we had met with a tiger. We turned in the opposite direction and ran away. We approached another house and tried once more.

The lady of this house after hearing our knock opened the door immediately, but when she saw that the knockers were girls, the expression on her face immediately changed from welcome to displeasure. We learnt later on that her daughter-in-law was giving birth to a child. It was a superstition of the country that if a man came to the house at the time, then the new-born baby would be a son, therefore we were not welcome.

'Elderly madam, could we stay the night here? We have lost our train.'

'No, my daughter-in-law is going to have a baby and we are very busy and cannot possibly take you in. You had better go to another house.'

'It is very late now, and we do not know the roads. In the dark the dogs are very fierce and will bite us. Where can we go? Please elderly madam, tell us where we can go.'

Either it was because she took pity on us, or else that she wanted to be sure of getting rid of us, but she sent somebody to take us to a shop which was kept by a widow and her daughter.

We were treated as two monsters dropped down suddenly from the sky, and many villagers came to surround us and stare at us. I was specially suspicious when I saw strange looking men staring at us, and when they whispered to each other I suspected they were planning some mischief.

I said in English to Shu Yun:

'We must not sleep to-night in case something unexpected happens.' She nodded her head and looked at me with a bitter smile.

Strangely enough, while we were suspicious in case they were not respectable people, they on their side suspected that we were bad women. Alas, there will always be misunderstandings between man and man.

Our hostess was really very hospitable. She cooked us an evening meal and made beds on two cupboards for us to sleep. As these were in the same room as the mother and daughter, our minds were really at ease. However, we did not sleep a wink that night, but kept on talking to each other until daylight. In the morning I found that I had a silver dollar in my pocket, and I presented it to the hostess for the hospitality of the night.

Like two truants going back to their school, we walked demurely towards the foreign building near the station. A man in uniform with dark spectacles came from one of the rooms and asked us:

'Are you the two girl students who passed the examination for the Central Military and Political School? Did you come from the train leaving Changsha at two o'clock yesterday afternoon, and did you miss the train here?'

'Yes. How did you know?'

Now we heaved a deep sigh of relief, and from our minds a very heavy weight was removed.

'Oh! Why didn't you come and report here earlier? You made us ring up every station to locate where you were, and we have sent people about to look for you. Go and wait on the platform. The express from Changsha will arrive almost immediately. You mustn't miss it this time.'

We made repeated deep bows of ninety degrees to him, who we were later to learn was the station-master. He did not return our salute, for he had already gone back to his office to telephone a report saying that we were found.

When we got into the train we saw Mr. Li, one of the students who was in our party, and asked him:

'Hey, why are you here?'

We were overjoyed, and shouted to him. He replied:

'Commissioner Chiu sent me to look for you two. He said that you two were the best students who passed the examination and no matter what happened you must be found.'

'Ha, ha!' Shu and I laughed and laughed. Who would have thought that these two 'best' students were such miserable fools?

CHAPTER XVIII

EXPELLED AGAIN

WHAT could be more comic in the world? Before I went into this new school I was expelled. It was almost unbelievable.

Here are the facts:

The Committee of the entrance examination had originally determined to take one hundred boy and twenty girl students, but as there were more than two thousand candidates and all their papers were so good, and as they had received many petitions from the candidates to increase the number of students, they at last decided to take two hundred boys and fifty girls.

But who would have thought that when we arrived at Wu Chang the matter would be changed? It was stated that according to instructions from higher up the establishment of this school was to train revolutionary soldiers out of the people of every province, therefore the number from each province should be the same. Now, the province of Hunan had taken more students than its share, therefore the number of students had to be reduced accordingly. They only wanted one hundred boys and twenty girls and no more, so they decided to have another examination and eliminate the rest.

When this news reached us we were as sorrowful as if we had been condemned to death. It seemed as if a piece of black cloth had been placed before our eyes and our bright future had suddenly become dark.

'No, none of us should be eliminated. We should be admitted to the school *en bloc*.' This was suggested by someone, and everyone agreed.

'Yes, let us protest against this second examination. We demand that we shall be admitted to the school unconditionally.'

We gathered together and I shouted this aloud.

'This is really a joke. If they want revolutionary people to be trained for work, the numbers should be the more the better. The only worry is that there aren't enough of them. How can they say that they want to decrease the number of revolutionary people?

If the students of Hunan province are so enthusiastic about throwing away their pens and joining the Army, it proves that they are all people of ideas and have the spirit of sacrifice. They have a profound understanding of revolution. This is a thing which should be encouraged, and from the revolutionary point of view they should take all these young people and train them to serve the country, so that they can help the suffering masses.

'Now, it seems that the Government is acting in the opposite direction. They want to reduce the number of people who want to join the Revolution, and say it is best to send them back to school to study their books. They say they want to develop the revolutionary influence on an average basis, but in reality they are obstructing the advance of the revolutionary youth. None of us must be eliminated! Whatever happens, we must all be admitted to the school together.'

This speech was loudly applauded, and another girl, whose nickname was 'Big Sister Iron,' said in a very husky voice:

'My schoolmates and my sisters, when we decided to join the Army we decided to sacrifice ourselves. We severed relations with our families to serve the Revolution. Our aim was not only to save our suffering selves but also the oppressed masses. Especially when we girls joined the Army it was a history-making event without any precedent. Since the Government gave an equal chance to the girls, enabling us to work for the nation and for society, it has been a blessing to women. While we were all so happy about this, the announcement that nearly two hundred of our numbers would be sent back was a fatal blow. I appeal to you, my sisters. We must protest against being sent back. What can we do if we go back? Our families will not recognise us as their daughters and our schools will not take us back as their students. We have nowhere to go. We have the spirit of revolution and we have the determination to sacrifice, but we are not being given a chance and there is no place for us. But in revolution there is only advance and no retreat. We must never turn back. Every one of us must go into the Military School.'

After this speech everybody was more than ever determined to protest against the second examination, and so in five minutes a committee to end the second examination was formed. On that very afternoon all of us went over the Yangtze River to Hankow to petition the Military Council, the secretary-in-chief of which was

General Tang San-Chi. All the students stood in formation outside the Government building, and the petition paper was handed in by ten representatives.

Of course, the verbal answer we received was fairly satisfactory and helpful. General Tang at once promised to send a wire to Nanking asking for further instructions, and in the meantime he promised that he would do his best so as to enable us to train for revolutionary purposes.

Three days went by and no news came. On the fourth day, early in the morning, a boy student came to the hotel where the girls were staying. He said:

'Woe to us, woe to us! Most of the students from Hunan have already gone to attend the second examination. Those who refused to be examined again will never be allowed to enter the school, and above all, the ten representatives have been expelled, according to a notice just made public.'

'What, the representatives expelled! Then I . . . I . . .'

It was like a thunderbolt in the middle of the night. I was dumbfounded. Although I knew that being selected as a representative I was acting in the interests of all, and if I should be sacrificed I would have no regret, nevertheless there was an indescribable sorrow in my mind.

On the next day it was reported in the newspapers that the Hunan students attended the second examination, and that the representatives had been expelled. When I saw my name in the report I felt very sorrowful. I realised that if I failed to join the Army this time, there would be no other way for me. Though my school might take me back, my mother would force me to marry, and I would have no chance to continue my studies but my life would be swallowed up by the monster of the old-fashioned society. As for my wish to serve the Revolution, it would never come to me again. This was the end. All my hopes were gone. Despair, despair! The extensive Tung Ting lake perhaps might be the place to drown myself.

While I was lamenting my fate my second elder brother saw the news of my expulsion. He tried his best to comfort me and was very anxious to help me. First he went to the Military School to see the acting president, and asked him to help me, but all the reply he got was: 'I cannot help. The orders came from above and they will never take them back.'

4 *

'But my younger sister is really a courageous girl. If you don't allow her to join the Revolution it will be a great pity. You must try to help her.' My second elder brother never gave up his entreaties.

'No, the only way is to let her enlist for the political class.'

Disappointed, my second elder brother came back with this news.

The political class was specially organised by General Tang. Because he had promised to help us, and had then received the order from Nanking that the second examination must take place to eliminate more than one hundred students, he thought it would be a pity to send us back and so he had specially established this political class for the rejected students. The term of the training was eight months, and the classes were held in Hankow. Big Sister Iron and other expelled representatives, together with all those who did not pass the second examination, all went to enlist for this political class, but I refused to do so, and waited to see what my second elder brother could do for me.

'Hurrah, my younger sister! There is a way out.' My second elder brother rushed in as happy as anything. 'A large number of students come from the North, where they cannot hold examinations, so they are examined here. If you change to a new name and say that you come from the North, you could be one of the Northern candidates.'

This was a rare chance, but also risky. If the school authorities found out that I was an expelled student, the situation would go from bad to worse. But I was determined to become a soldier, and was willing to take any risks. I took my photograph with me and went to enlist. My name I gave as Hsieh Ping-Ying, and for my native place I put down Peking.

'Where is your school certificate? Haven't you got it with you?' a clerk in uniform asked me seriously.

'No, I haven't. Don't you know that all we students from the North, being under the control of the military lords, had to leave in secret? Many of us have no certificates.'

I thought this excuse very sound, but another clerk asked me:

'Are you from Peking? You have a marked Hunan accent.' My heavens! He seemed to know my secret!

'Yes, I was born in Peking, but I spent most of my childhood in Hunan.' Although I tried to be very calm in appearance, my heart went pit-a-pat. All the clerks seemed to be suspicious of me, and I was quite ready to escape in despair.

Suddenly I realised that the room was crowded with other students who wanted to enlist, and I quickly made way for them to come forward.

On the day of the examination I, the only Southerner, was mixing with more than a thousand Northerners. But when I heard everybody talking with a northern accent I felt I was in North China. Nearly all of them, boys and girls, were big hefty people, with coarse dark skins, and full of robust beauty. I liked their faces, which were kindly and full of smiles. My first impression of the Northerners was that they were sincere, genuine and honest.

My temperament is exactly like the Northerners, but in appearance I looked just their opposite. I am small in stature and have a paler skin, and above all I cannot speak with a northern accent. Otherwise I just felt that I was one of them.

Either because I did my papers very hurriedly, or because the questions in the examination were very easy, on those two days I was always the first to hand in my papers. The examiners seemed to pay special attention to me, and whenever I handed in my papers at the desk they would always stare at me, and I was afraid that probably they knew my secret. Until the result was known I felt as if I was sitting on a cushion of pins.

'Congratulations! congratulations! You have passed first on the list!' When a friend gave me this news I could scarcely believe my ears. I thought he was joking with me. Even if I had only succeeded in being the last on the list I would have been more than happy. Full of excitement, I went to see the list. It was in the Academy of Hunan and Hupeh. I raised my eyes and actually saw that I was first, and I cannot possibly describe how happy I was.

A soldier! In a few days I should be a soldier, and my new life would begin. Hurrah!

That night my second elder brother treated me to wine and special dishes, and also invited a few other friends to join in the celebration. I, who had been expelled, was now admitted at the top of the list. It was a joy of which I had never dreamt.

Chapter XIX

SERVING IN THE RANKS

This, of course, I remember very clearly. On the 25th of November 1926, in the afternoon we moved into the Central Military and Political School and were quartered in the girl students' department. The moment we entered that building we saw many groups of young ladies dressed in delicate coloured garments whispering to each other. What they were saying I could not tell, though their faces expressed sorrow and disappointment. There was one who was secretly wiping her tears with her sleeve.

'Why do you cry? You needn't be sorry. If you cannot go out to-day, we will see what we can do to-morrow.' This was whispered to her by a friend.

When I heard this I knew that it was about leaving the school.

'What is the matter? Is it that all those who came in to-day are not allowed to go out again?' I said to someone who had come in before me.

'Yes. Nobody is allowed to go out again.'

'Then perhaps to-morrow?'

'Nor to-morrow. I heard that we are allowed to go out once a month.'

I wished I had not asked her. Otherwise it would not have disturbed me so much. We all thought that if we could just leave our luggage in first, later on we could go back to our hotel again, and have a farewell supper. Besides, we had left a few odds and ends to be collected later on. If we were only allowed to go out once a month we had as good as entered a prison. While we were talking about this kind of imprisonment, a little bugler boy of about 14 or 15 came to us and blew:

'Te-te-te, ta-ta-te-ta.'

Very soon three officers in uniform came out. Among them one was a woman, but that could only be distinguished after careful examination because there was no difference in their dress. While I was looking at them like this, I suddenly heard one of the officers shout:

'To formation!'

Crowding, crowding, crowding, we rushed together, and soon we got into formation by ourselves, with the tall and short ones all mixed together. Some of the girls, to whom the female officer looked ridiculous, began to giggle.

'Quick, quick, get into formation, and don't laugh.'

The officer was very severe in his appearance, and we all shuddered a little.

We stood there for nearly an hour before we were divided into three formations, according to our height. I was the thirty-third of the third division, for most of them were much taller than I, and there were only ten or a dozen girls who were slightly shorter than I. I patted the shoulder of the girl next to me.

'You are too small. How can you shoulder a heavy rifle?'

'Ha, ha! You think you are very big yourself. Don't you know that you are just a tiny soldier like myself?'

'Stop talking!' That was our first warning. We looked at each other and still smiled a bit, and felt we were getting something more than we had bargained for.

Soon five men carrying two parcels of uniforms each came out from the building, and as the officer called the roll, each of us was given a suit of uniform in grey cotton, a military hat, a pair of shoes with rubber soles, a pair of straw sandals, two pairs of black socks, a pair of putees in grey cloth, and a leather belt about two inches in width. When these things were distributed, the officer—whom we later learnt was a lieutenant—instructed us how to put on the putees and the leather belt, and how to salute.

'Go to your dormitories immediately and throw away your fine ladies' clothes. Put on the uniform, and from to-day onwards you are no longer delicate ladies but girl soldiers.'

When we heard this we burst out into loud laughter. The lieutenant did not scold us, but his fierce looks stopped our laughter. He went on:

'Most important of all, you must wash away your rouge and powder, not leaving a trace of them on your faces. All your hair should be cut short. If you can shave it all off, like the men, all the better.'

'Oh!' we all exclaimed in alarm, but the lieutenant looked fiercer than before and all his kind demeanour was gone.

'You must realise in the first place that in coming here you are not entering a comfortable school, where you are still regarded as delicate ladies. You are now soldiers, and from to-day onwards you must learn the duty of a soldier, which is to obey and to serve.'

As soon as we heard this we were encouraged, and truly enough, from that day onwards, we considered ourselves soldiers and began to discard our former silly habits.

When we were dismissed we went to our dormitories to change into the uniform, and these were some of the remarks I heard among my fellow-students:

"To discard our furs will really be very cold!'

'This hat is a disgrace!'

'I have never seen such a pair of socks in my life!'

'Ai . . . Ya . . . This uniform is too big for me. I look like a character in a puppet show!'

This made us laugh again.

In twenty minutes we were all transformed into rough but sprightly soldiers.

For the first time we went to the dining-room in formation, and we were ordered to finish our meal in ten minutes. If you have finished it earlier, you were not allowed to go out of the dining-room by yourself but must wait until the end of the ten minutes, when the officer on duty would shout 'Attention!' and then you must stand up. Then you went out in formation to the open ground to be dismissed there.

In the evening Sergeant Chen, who was in charge of the girls, came to lecture us. He was a tall man of about forty years of age. He was thin, and his face was pock-marked. To exaggerate a little, his face looked like a pine-apple. His outward appearance seemed to tell us that he was a gentle and kind man, not at all like a soldier, but he made a different impression on us when he returned our salute by stretching out his five fingers as if he was going to slap our faces. One of us burst into laughter, and the rest were quite ready to follow, when suddenly his eyes gave us a very severe warning.

His voice was quite mild, but he had a pet phrase which would make anybody giggle. He began almost all his sentences and remarks with the phrase 'by the time.' For instance, he would say, 'By the time you have come here.' 'by the time you have resolved to sacrifice,' 'by the time you discard your romantic thoughts,' 'by the time you are not depending on others,' and 'by the time you are not lazy again,' and so on. Sometimes, when the sentence should begin with the phrase 'by the time,' then he would say 'by the time, by the time,' and we had to bite our lips in order to suppress our giggles.

After his lecture the roll was again called. We were told that this was earlier than ordinary bedtime, but because this was our first night and as we had to get up at 5.30 the next morning for morning drill, we were allowed to go to sleep a little earlier on that night.

Alas, how could we go to sleep? It was only eight o'clock and there were more than forty of us in one room. It was not furnished in any other way than with some hard boards for our beds, a grey blanket each as a mattress, and a coverlet over that. We had always been accustomed to sleeping on spring mattresses, and most of us were used to warm silk coverlets, so we were not at all comfortable.

'When the light is turned off, nobody is allowed to speak. Anybody caught speaking will be punished to-morrow!'

The political instructress came to inspect the dormitories, and the atmosphere was immediately tense. She looked at each bed by the light of a torch, and told us not to cover our heads with the coverlet and not to catch cold. In a way she was like our mother, looking after us.

We really came into a new world on that night.

'I am not dreaming? Why am I sleeping here?'

In the middle of the night I was awakened by the sound of the night watch. I opened my eyes and saw pale moonlight shining into the room from the windows. The room seemed to resemble the big common ward in a hospital, and I could hear the loud snoring of some of the occupants. I could not go to sleep again because I thought in a few hours time I should be shouldering a gun and become a soldier, shouting 'One, two, three, four' on the drill ground. When a person becomes too happy or too excited, he is unable to go to sleep all night. His mind is full of thoughts, just like millions of sparks dancing around him. In the quiet of the night I would have liked to shout and jump about.

The girl who slept next to me also woke up. She yawned, and asked me quietly:

'Do you know what time it is? Shall we get up soon?'

'Very soon. It is already past three o'clock.'

At first there were only two of us talking to each other, but by and by many others woke up and joined in. At last we all got up, because we had been told that we were only given ten minutes to dress, including making our beds, putting on our puttees and washing. So we decided to begin earlier, and just about four o'clock we were all on the drill ground.

'Hey, what is the matter? The bugle has not sounded, why did you all get up? Too early, too early! Go back to your dormitories and sleep. Don't stop here.'

Our lieutenant came to us. When he saw a group of dark shapes moving about on the parade ground he was very much surprised. He did not know that every one of us was there.

'No, officer! We dare not go to sleep again, in case the bugle should not waken us, so we decided to wait here on the parade ground for the bugle.' I made this reply, and at that time I did not realise that before you answer your superior you should click your heels, stand at attention, and begin your remarks by saying 'Report!'

'You are quite enthusiastic, which is a very good sign, but I hope you will maintain this kind of spirit always.'

Evidently he overlooked my lack of formality because it was the first time we had been in the school.

We began our life there by attending four classes in science and four classes in drill. A rifle is very heavy—I think it must be over thirty *catties*. There were six of the girls who were as short as Shu Yun, and though I wasn't much taller than they were, every time we went to drill we could not help smiling at them. When we were practising running, these girls could hardly bear the weight of their rifles. But that was only for the first few days. After a week of training we had all become short but smart soldiers. It is rather strange to realise that, although we had always been free and romantic and comfortable in our life, we did not feel it at all insufferable when we were suddenly thrust into life in the Army, where we had to obey and were trained in a mechanical way, and had to endure hardship. None of us thought of deserting because of this uncomfortable way of living. The only thing we felt to be at all inconvenient to us was that during the time of training, which was three months, after which we became proper soldiers, we were only allowed to go out once a month.

Winter came with big snowflakes on the roof. When other people were having sweet dreams in their comfortable beds, covered with snow-white sheets, we were impressing our footprints on the white snow and shouting 'One—two—one—two—one—two—three—four.'

CHAPTER XX

'DOWN WITH LOVE!'

As soon as we had learned to sing the song of 'Struggle,' everyone of us liked to hum all the time this chorus:

'Train quickly to become the vanguard of the people,
To wipe away the old ways, and down with love.
Accomplish the Socialist Revolution, you great women!'

And every time we sang the phrase 'Down with love!' we would always shout specially loudly, as if we wanted to warn all our friends that during the time of our mission we were not giving any thought to love.

The spring wind is soft and warm and intoxicating, and the Goddess of Spring brings sweet seeds of love with her which she spreads in the hearts of young men and women. But in the meantime there was the god who came to spread hot blood over the brave soldiers, male and female. With him came the harsh sound of the bugle, which wakened them from their dreams and told them to kill their enemies. We came out from rosy palaces and went towards the Socialist battleground, where many skeletons were laid. In this place were discarded our narrow ideas of life, which widened out to become a universal love for the oppressed people of the whole world, a life of comradeship.

Nevertheless, there were a few boy and girl comrades who were in love with each other, but there was one guiding principle before them. One must ask oneself first of all whether the lover was standing on the same side of the front, whether they were sincerely revolutionary and would sacrifice all for the cause. In short, their love must be a revolutionary love.

It only stands to reason that the girls who had been oppressed by the old moral code would look immediately for some kind of new thought when they had just come out from their iron cage. But in practice it was not so. Neither did they think that love was all important, nor had for them its mysteries. Their most urgent need was this—revolution. On revolution they had put their future and their happiness. They knew that unless the old system was completely shattered, womankind could never be freed. To create a happiness which could be enjoyed by all members of society was the most urgent need of mankind. Personal love is a private and selfish affair and is of no consequence. While we were all quite ready to sacrifice our lives for the welfare of the masses, we considered love as a plaything entirely belonging to the idle rich.

That was our thought and that was our understanding of love.

One early morning, during my second month of training, the officer on duty handed me a very thick letter. It was from *him*—that image which had haunted me in the days of my first love. I felt the letter to be very heavy, like a piece of lead in my hand. My friends looked at me and smiled, and they said it must be another sweet love letter from one of my admirers. At that time I was editing the daily paper of the Military School, and consequently I used to receive letters very often. When I looked at the handwriting on the envelope, I felt as if my hand had touched an electric wire. My mind was absorbed and I felt uneasy, but I anxiously waited until we were dismissed and then I went to a corner of the parade ground to read the letter.

Good heavens, what was he doing! The notepaper was full of bloodstains, the handwriting was awful. I had no courage to finish the letter and hurriedly put it into my pocket. Had the letter come a few months ago I would have treasured it above all things in the world, but now, alas, I had no time for such things. I had dedicated my life to the masses. The complete trend of my thought was now altered.

I would really have liked to tear this letter into a thousand pieces, or to burn it so that nothing of it would be left, but conflicting thoughts again entered my mind and at last I was impelled to re-open the letter and to read its passionate words.

He hoped that I would accept his earnest love and he would like to join me for ever, wherever I might go.

While I was in a dilemma, the sound of the bugle came to me, and I ran to the training ground.

'Whose love letter is that?' Shu Yun asked me in a whisper.

'No.' I shook my head resolutely, but I was almost in tears.

Shu Yun was my best friend, and we had no secrets from each other. On that night I showed her the blood-stained letter, and she said:

'Alas, what a pity that he is not one of our comrades!'

It was from reliable sources that we knew he was acting contrary to our cause. Alas, what was there to be said? This was the end.

Prompted by my sentiments, I eventually wrote an answer to him, asking him to come to Wu Chang immediately to join us in our work. But the letter was gone for a month, then for two months, and still no reply came. I realised that his letter must have been prompted by his temporary feelings, and that nothing could change his ideals. I could not possibly love a man who was not my comrade. I must banish his image from my mind for ever. In fact, he was one of my enemies, and I should treat him with cruelty. This was a time when we should place reason before sentiment. If our cause was the same, then we could be friends, otherwise we must be enemies. Finished was my dream of first love, banished was that adorable image, banished for ever.

Chapter XXI

SOME POINTS ON DISCIPLINE

ONE of the boys was nicknamed 'The Lunatic,' but he was really a humorist. He was a very silent fellow, and sometimes he would not say a word during the whole course of the day, but his appearance made him look like a lunatic and induced people to laugh at him. He had a very strange way of moving his eyes slowly and by so doing he would make us laugh.

One day, when the captain was working busily at his desk he heard somebody shouting outside 'Report!' The voice was very urgent and the captain put down his pen and shouted back 'Come in!'

The Lunatic stepped in and made his salute. The captain looked at him and asked him what he had to report. The Lunatic came forward, took a teapot from the desk and drank like a thirsty cow who had come to a pool of clear water.

'Hey, what are you doing!'

The captain was angry, and was on the point of striking the Lunatic.

'Report! I have finished!' He saluted the captain and turned to go away.

The captain did not know whether to laugh or to be angry, and shouted loudly 'Devil! devil!'

Another time, when all of us were in the gymnasium to be inspected by our commander-in-chief, and after the officer on duty had made the preliminary report, the Lunatic, with his rifle on his shoulder, came straight to the commander-in-chief and shouted loudly and hurriedly: 'Report!'

'What!'

'Report! I want to go to the lavatory.'

There was an uproar, and even the commander-in-chief could not help smiling, but it was well known that he was a lunatic, otherwise he would have been severely punished.

He was a very artistic person and could draw very well. All the slogan posters were decorated by him, and because of this he was well liked by the officers. Sometimes his actions and his words were a little out of the ordinary, but when they found him to be too much out of control he was shut up in prison for a short period.

A girl soldier, Yun Chen, liked to powder her face slightly, and paid extraordinary attention to her dress. Once she went out to meet her lover and exceeded her time of leave. On her return she was locked up and on the first day was not allowed to eat rice or to drink water. Although those who kept watch outside the jail were her schoolmates, orders were orders and nobody dared to give her anything to eat. If anybody dared to have a peep at her by passing the place, the officer on duty would pull a long face and say:

'Do you want to go in there, too? We will put you in another one, if you like.'

She was shut up for three days and there was no news of her release. We were sorry for her and felt that the lieutenant was a little too severe in her punishment. For a first offence more leniency should have been shown. We learned that she was only allowed to sleep on a hard board with a grey blanket over her, and had two bowls of rice and a bowl of water for her daily fare. I ventured to ask the lieutenant whether some vegetables could be given her, but he said:

'No. A soldier who has acted contrary to discipline must be treated in this way. She is now a prisoner and should suffer that kind of hardship. If you give her nice things to eat, then there is no sense in punishment.'

'When will she be released?'

'If she confesses her guilt, she will be freed to-morrow.'

Originally she was to be confined for three days, but because she was obstinate and would not confess her guilt she was imprisoned for two days more. At the end of the fifth day she used some impolite words to the lieutenant, and so she had to stay in prison for another two days. When we heard that Yun Chen was to be in prison for seven days, we all became cautious ourselves, feeling that one day we would taste something like that. When she was released she looked much paler and was not so lively as before.

As military orders are as weighty as mountains and party discipline is as hard as iron, I, too, had to be punished some three times. But they were not serious offences, and once I was told to stand facing the wall for an hour because I left the table at meal-time, and two other times I was punished for small offences. Once it was found by the lieutenant that I had been drawing ducks, little cats, little dogs, drums and bugles carelessly on my desk. He scolded me severely and said:

'Romantic literary people are not fit for the work of revolution.'

After this I began to be different. I had with me some fiction which I liked, but I now threw it away and took only *Farmers' Revolution*, *History of Revolution*, books on Economics, Politics and Military Science. I think I could recite the whole book of the *Principles of Infantry Training*.

But, as the old saying is, 'It is easy to change the shape of a mountain and to alter the course of a river, but it is difficult to change the nature of man.' Therefore how could I suppress my feelings, especially as I had a very obstinate nature? My childish ways could never be entirely suppressed. I remember once when we were holding manœuvres in the country, I dashed to a buffalo and sat on his back as soon as I heard the bugle sound 'Dismiss!' The sergeant who was in charge of us was very angry with me, but I said smilingly to him:

'Report! As there are no horses in our school for us to practise on, I must use this buffalo instead!'

Chapter XXII

SETTING OUT

ALL of a sudden we had an order saying that twenty girls were to be picked out to organise a publicity party to join the Northern Punitive Expedition. Our objective was Honan.

'Report! I want to join the expedition!'

'Report! I am a Northerner. I am specially suitable for publicity work with the Northern people.'

'Report! I am very robust. I want to join the expedition.'

The lieutenant's room was as busy as a beehive with so many of us going in and coming out.

'You all stop! We all have to join in the expedition sooner or later, but this time I need only twenty of you who are specially robust, or can run very quickly and write or make up public speeches. Those who are not selected will have a chance later on.'

Each one of us hoped that she would be selected. I was particularly happy because I thought I was the best. I could run and I could scribble a little bit. Surely I would be selected.

Next morning, when the lieutenant was reading out the names of those to go to Honan, my name came second. My heavens, I hoped I was not wrong! There was no other Hsieh Ping-Ying among the girls. I was nearly crazy with joy. As soon as we were dismissed I went to pack my things and to write a letter to my third elder brother telling him of my departure. On the third day he came to see me. I was surprised and happy to see him.

'I received your letter last night. It was written in such an heroic manner that I gave it immediately to the printers to be set up in type so that it could be published in my paper. I immediately left for the station to catch the 8.30 to come here to see you.' There was a tremor in his voice and the tears were not far from his eyes. I was afraid that it would be infectious, so I turned my eyes away to the slogan poster, 'A Revolutionary should not shed tears but only shed blood.'

'Our second elder brother is probably in Honan now. I think I am sure to meet him there. My third elder brother, I think you had better go too. If we could all meet in the front line, how happy we should be!' I forced a smile when I said this to him.

'The news that you are setting out has been kept from our family. I am sure that if our parents knew that you are going they would be very sorry indeed.'

I cannot explain, but I felt that my heart was as hard as a stone. Instead of feeling sorrowful, I felt happy and excited.

'Could you get leave so that you can come out with me to have a drink?'

'No. Now that we are soon to set out we should adhere to discipline more strictly.'

'Well, I had better get back to Chandsha immediately.'

'All right. We will have a drink when I return after the victory.'

Bidding me farewell, he went away with tears in his eyes. When my schoolmate, who was on duty at the door, saluted him, he forgot to return the salute.

Waiting, waiting, waiting! The day for us to set out never came. Those twenty girls who were selected were very anxious to go, but nothing happened. Suddenly a very urgent order came saying that the enemy was now near Ting Su Bridge, and that we should all set out for battle, as otherwise our enemy might come to Wu Chang.

On that very night our commander-in-chief lectured us in the dormitory. We were organised into the Central Independent Division, and all of us set out next morning, except about thirty girls who were left behind to look after the publicity and nursing work.

At five o'clock in the morning we were ready. Outside the door of the girls' quarters it was like a seething river. Thousands of people crowded there to see us and bid us farewell. Among the excited and huge crowd there were one or two elderly ladies who were crying and shouting to the officials:

'My girl cannot go to fight. I have only one daughter.'

'My girl cannot go. If she dies, I will die too.'

It was a very noisy place. You could hear the sound of bugles, laughter, crying and shouting.

'Elderly lady, do not be down-hearted, we will come back victorious.'

'Elderly lady, do not trouble about your daughter. We all have parents. Why should you cry?'

'Forward, march!'

The formation started out amidst loud cheers and to the sound of the bugles.

'Kill the enemy and come back in victory!' Loud shouting came to us from the crowd. 'Kill the enemy and come back in victory!'

We shouted back to them, and it was in this spirit that we went to the battle-field.

Fierce fighting was going on at the Ting Su Bridge. When I looked out of the train on which we were travelling, I saw there were wounded comrades covered with blood lying on stretchers. They looked tragic, and sometimes their faint cries were more tragic than their looks. I also saw dead people, and soldiers who had lost their limbs. Some of the girls wanted to get permission from the sergeant to leave the train and give first aid to the wounded, and some offered to bury the dead.

'No, the train will start immediately. There is more important work in front for us to do. The first aid people will come and attend to them here very soon.' Our sergeant said this with dignity, which made us feel more heroic than ever. I began to realise the cruelty and horror of war.

For three days we had never had a proper meal. We had started at six o'clock after a very hurried breakfast, and then we had to march until eight or nine o'clock at night before we stopped to eat something. Now that we were marching forward we began to know that the life of a soldier is the most terrible of any for human beings, and we were considered fortunate if we got from time to time some very coarse rice with the husks on, which was sure to be mixed with a lot of sand and dust. As for anything to go with the rice, these things were lacking because they were not very easy to carry. In most cases it was just a handful of strong-smelling preserved beans sprinkled with salt. Under ordinary circumstances these things would not have gone down our throats, but strange to relate, when we were really hungry we enjoyed the coarse rice and strong-smelling beans better than chicken, fish or meat. They went down our throats quicker than the best of rice, and the only trouble was that we did not have enough of them.

The month of June is the time when men die of the heat. Perspiration like rain ran down our cheeks and our backs, and our clothes soon became as wet as if we had been plunged into water. We felt as if the soles of our feet were walking on hot stones, and the skin was peeling from our faces. 'Hot! Devilishly hot!' was heard everywhere. But we were not dismayed, nor would we turn back or desert. Every one of us was willing to endure present sufferings, looking for a happier time when our victory should come. Sometimes a pail of dirty, muddy water would serve us not only to wash in, but to wash our clothes and also to quench our thirst. Sometimes it would only ooze out as a swampy pool. This kind of life seemed to be full of meaning and full of interest, and I began to write my diary of the war.

During the time of our forward march I would snatch a few minutes now and again, either in the day-time when we were taking a short rest, or I would sacrifice a short while during our times for sleeping, and by the light of an oil lamp, which was very dim, I would write down the happenings of the day, using a wretched pen and whatever paper I could get hold of, and using one of my knees as a writing-desk. I intended to send these pages of my diary to the literary editor of the *Central Daily News*, that long-bearded old man, Mr. Sun Fu Yuan, but unfortunately one day my little bundle containing my blanket, my water-bottle and my food box, all disappeared while I was away for a short time. At first I thought it must be one of my schoolmates who had taken it for me, but later on, after I had enquired from everybody in turn and none of them knew anything of it, I realised at last that it was gone. It was very hard on me, because I had suffered many difficulties to write that diary, and as I never had time to read what I had written I could not remember what was in it. Because of this unfortunate incident, and because of our forced marches, which averaged from eighty to a hundred and twenty *li* a day, I was never able to continue to write. Although I had written a few letters about this march, I kept no detailed records of the life of that time.

I had a very queer habit. Whatever I had written once, I hated to write a second time. Even when I could remember very distinctly what I saw and did, I would not record it once more. Therefore a second diary of the war could never be written.

Chapter XXIII

AN INCIDENT ON THE ROAD

WHEN our army arrived at a place somewhere near Hung-Ko and Shan-Lin, a crowd of organised farmers was following our formation, and with them were three prisoners. These were three rich rogues who had oppressed the poor people before the Revolution. At night when we stopped at this place, these three men were shut in a dark room, and all the good farmers were crazy with happiness. They all shouted:

'Ha, ha! we never dreamt that the day would come for us to settle our account with them!'

A boy of fourteen or fifteen was on watch, and he had a stick with him. He looked fiercely at the three prisoners. The three men were perspiring and panting, but in their eyes there was still a flame of cruelty, to show that they must have been very powerful persons in times of peace. One of them had a fine beard, and he had been arrested in a temple forty *li* from here. He pretended to cry and appealed to us.

'Why do you cry? Do you think anybody will have sympathy with you?' one of the farmers cried. 'Ha, ha! so we have got this old rascal at last. This is a happy moment indeed.'

'Officer, please. These three people were oppressing us farmers before the Revolution. I hope you will shoot them.' The leader of the Farmers' Union addressed our lieutenant.

'They will be properly tried before they are condemned,' was the brief reply from our lieutenant.

'Before the Revolution the lives of all the people in the village were in their hands, and to-day their lives are in our hands. Nevertheless, we will give them a fair trial.'

All the villagers came to see these three prisoners. There were men, women, old men, boys and girls, and on all their faces were smiles and happiness. They all wanted to have just one peep into the dark room, as if to make sure that they had got these dangerous people safe and that they had no means of escaping again.

'Comrades, please go back. We want to have our supper now. You can leave the prisoners in our care,' the little bugler boy stood up and said to the crowd. Then he took up his bugle and gave the signal for supper.

'My comrades, you may all go to your supper. I will watch these prisoners for you,' offered one of the farmers.

'All right, and I will join you,' added another farmer.

While we were having supper the villagers went to another part of the ground to have a mass meeting. They had selected a jury, and they also passed a resolution demanding the lives of the three rogues. They elected their own prosecuting counsel. As soon as the mass meeting ended, the crowd dispersed, and the head of the village came to speak to our lieutenant.

'Comrade, please keep a careful watch over the three men. If they escape we will have no end of trouble because they are the three most dangerous people in this part of the country.'

Our lieutenant assured him that he need not worry, and that by to-morrow they would be tried and sentence would be passed if they were found guilty.

I was charged to keep watch on that night. Originally that was not my duty, but the girl who should have kept watch was called away to do an urgent job elsewhere and I was put in her place. I was very happy to do this. In ordinary times I would not have been willing to keep watch at night if it was dark, as I would be imagining that ghosts were coming near me. But to-night I was very brave and in high spirits. I felt as if these three prisoners had been captured by me, and there was a feeling of satisfaction when, shouldering my rifle, I walked to and fro guarding the door of the prisoners' room.

The elderly man with the white beard made an awful face at me and appealed to me:

'Officer, please set me free. I am a good man and they were wrong to arrest me.'

The second prisoner was as thin as a bundle of dried sticks. He was about forty years of age and of very small stature. He knelt before me and knocked his head on the ground:

'Officer, please have pity on me. There are more than twenty people in my family and they are all dependent on me. If I die, they will all die. I am not a rogue as they said. Please deliver me, officer, please save me!'

The third one was a short-sighted man, and his teeth were all black with the marks of opium smoking. He also came and knelt down to me, asking me to free him. I had to turn away and not look at them, but they would not let me alone.

After they had been entreating me for some time, I said:

'Don't call me officer. I am only a soldier on night duty. Don't say anything. Other people are sleeping and you mustn't disturb them.'

I had never addressed such harsh words to anybody before, but at that time, when I looked at these prisoners and heard how powerful and cruel they had been in former days, I only regretted that I could not treat them more fiercely than I did. They all knew that I was a woman soldier and probably, thinking that a woman would have a softer heart, they tried their best to appeal to me.

'Help them!' I thought to myself. 'I wonder how many lives they have taken before the Revolution! Besides, they must have oppressed the farmers very much, otherwise the whole village would not have turned against them.'

'Officer on watch, I am really an honest man. I have never done anything wrong in my life. You may go and investigate in the neighbouring village. If my own villagers have some grudge against me, you mustn't believe their words.'

'There is no need for investigation. If a person has been arrested by the people of his own village, it is enough proof that he must be a very bad man.'

'It was only because I once punished the pock-marked Wong, and now he has been elected chief of the village he has arrested me in revenge. You must save me, officer.'

These were the words of the very small man.

'The Revolutionary Army would not allow anybody to take a private revenge, but you have been arrested with the consent of all the people of the village. If several hundred people thought you to be a rascal, there could be no question of a private revenge. You must shut up!'

He was silent, but the opium smoker shouted again:

'Aio, my bonds are tight! Officer, please be very merciful. Untie my hands.'

'Shut up, don't move. If you try to make any trouble I will report you to the officer, and he may shoot you now.'

My threat frightened them. They still murmured, but did not shout.

At twelve o'clock the lieutenant came to have an inspection. He looked over the room with his torchlight and seemed surprised.

'Hey, where is the elderly man with the beard?'

Alas, he was not to be seen. I was frightened to death, but at last found him crouching in a dark corner. I was relieved.

'Ah, that is good. Now, you keep a very good watch and do not fall asleep. If any one of them escapes you have to answer for it.'

'Yes, sir,' I answered, and he went away.

The bright full moon was like a disc of jade hanging in the middle of the sky. The hot air had become cool again, and a gentle breeze was wafted across my face. In the room next to that of the prisoners there were several members of the Women's League of the village. They were not sleeping, but talking.

'It was outrageous! He said that his wife should not join the Women's League, and when she came back he gave her a severe beating.'

'How do you know?'

'One of her neighbours came to tell me. His wife was too afraid of him to report. We sent eight people to arrest him but he had already escaped.'

'I don't think he could have gone very far. You should look carefully in the neighbourhood.'

'There is no need for your advice. We have looked everywhere, and nowhere could he be found.'

I was so interested in their talk that I peeped in, and I found that they were working at a desk, writing despatches all the time. It seems that in this time of war the people of the village were working in two shifts, and these women were working all night.

Perhaps I was too tired, but at last I sat down on the ground. According to Army discipline, this was against the rules, but my legs were tired, and it seemed that the person who should be on duty after me would never turn up and I was doing more than my share. To sit on the cool soil was very comfortable, but my eyes were tired, and I dared not give them any rest. I was only hoping that an officer would turn up to inspect for the night, or even better, one of my schoolmates would come and relieve me. However, I kept a very careful watch with my tired eyes on these three people, as I was afraid that they might manage to untie each other. The room used for their prison was not meant for that purpose, and if they were strong men they could easily get out.

'Officer, I am very thirsty, please give me some water.' That was a little scheme of the bearded man.

'Shut up! When daylight comes you will have something to drink.'

'I cannot wait until daylight, officer. Please be merciful and fetch me some water to drink.'

'No, I cannot leave here.'

'Not even if we are going to die? You mustn't let us suffer from thirst or hunger.'

I never thought that this opium smoker was so cunning.

'This is no time to give you a drink. You will have plenty of water when somebody comes to relieve me.'

The small man was very near to me and entreated me out of kindness to try and get some water for them. I knew that it was a trick to get me away, and I refused to do their bidding.

Early next morning there was a big meeting in the open ground. The whole village turned out, and on a platform there stood the representatives of the Farmers' Union. Our lieutenant acted as judge, but there was not a man who would consent to be their defender. The representative of the Farmers' Union put forward their case, and demanded that they should be condemned to death. All their cruel deeds were read out, and there was not a single dissentient among the jury or among the crowd asking that their lives should be spared. On the contrary, so impatient were the crowd that they kept on shouting:

'Shoot them! Shoot them! Quick! Quick!'

After the demand had been put forward to sentence them to death, the foreman of the jury, a hefty dark man with piercing large black eyes and an impressive commanding voice, whom I at once recognised to be a man who had come several times the night before to look at these prisoners, stood up and said:

'We find that Wang Fu Tsai, Kuo Shiu Kong, and Wang Shin Shon are guilty of all the crimes just mentioned, but we do not want to decide the matter only by ourselves. We propose to let all those present cast their votes as to whether they should be condemned to death or not. Will you please all consider yourselves as members of the jury, and please raise your hands if you are in favour of saying they are guilty, like we did.'

'We do! We do!' shouted the crowd with one voice and every hand was raised.

'As a matter of formality, all those who think they are not guilty please raise their hands.'

All hands went down. He then informed the judge, our lieutenant, of the decision, and the judge passed sentence on them.

Very soon these three men were shot.

CHAPTER XXIV

NIGHT MARCH

AT eight o'clock that night we received orders from the Divisional Headquarters that we were to be moved to a place called Chin San An, about forty *li* from Hung-Ko. According to a secret report, there was a small company of the enemy hiding themselves on the mountain. Our forward march at night would probably bring us in touch with the enemy. This night march was the first we had since our departure from Wu Chang.

'You people probably have been accustomed to the easy life of your schooldays, and being tired, as you are, will think it an unendurable hardship. But you must remember that you are soldiers marching to the battle-field. You must prepare yourselves for any kind of hardship, and even the sacrifice of your lives must not deter you from going forward. I now want to tell you that the object of the night march is to avoid detection by our enemy, and also because the order is very urgent, we must reach our objective within twelve hours. The mountain pass which we are going to take is not very easy to travel, and above all, we must not use torches. You will have to walk very carefully, slowly and bravely. If you should fall down, which no doubt you will very often do in the course of the night, do not make a fuss about it but get up as quickly and as lightly as you can, and proceed without interruption. Everyone should hold their rifle steadily, and not knock their water-pot and food-box together to make a noise. Remember your discipline. Do not talk with each other, and do not walk too heavily. Your footsteps should be as light as those of a mouse. . . .'

When our lieutenant said that we all burst into laughter.

'Hey, before you start you break discipline by laughing. If anybody dares to laugh while we are marching, that will be considered as acting against my orders. It is quite possible that by a laugh you would convey to the enemy that you were there. That is a crime as bad as communicating with the enemy, and you know the penalty for that.' His exaggeration of this offence almost made us laugh again, but we dared not do so.

'The lieutenant was after all a man from the ranks. If he said that we should move forward as silently and swiftly as a swallow, it would be rather poetical.' I said this to a friend, and she laughed secretly.

We started to march in single file, and our little group of soldiers wriggled along like a snake. At first we could still hear the rattle of the water-bottles and food-boxes, but after repeated warnings from our sergeant we ceased to hear any noise at all, except that made by the new straw sandals, which gave out a series of sharp 'Ge gae, ge gae' sounds. The sergeant asked:

'Who is making that noise?'

'Report! I cannot help it. It is my new straw sandals, I bought them this morning. They are making a noise but I think it is rather melodious.'

But this reply was not appreciated by the sergeant.

'Do not talk nonsense. If I hear any noise again I will order you to walk on your bare feet.'

Of course nobody wanted to walk on bare feet, for the road was rough. From henceforth everybody was really walking as lightly as a mouse.

The night was dark, so dark that we could not see our own hands. Everybody was walking as carefully as if they were treading on thin ice. Suddenly, splash! a man fell into the ditch. Nobody dared to pause, and the man had to get up as quickly as he could.

'Quick, quick!' That was the sergeant's voice.

'I am wet, and covered with mud,' the man coming from the ditch said. 'I can scarcely open my eyes.'

'Then walk with closed eyes. You have to get along.'

Immediately everybody knew that somebody had had a ducking in the ditch, and we warned each other to be very careful of the place.

The road was really difficult. Sometimes we had to climb, and sometimes we heard a torrent somewhere near us, and one felt that if one fell into that, it would be the end. It was now a very dangerous road.

'Be careful, all those behind. There is a very big brook on your right side. Keep to the left and walk carefully. If you fall down you will not be able to get up again.' This warning was given by someone who walked in front.

When we heard there was a big brook, we became very anxious

immediately. The thought that if you fell down in the brook you might not get out again made you more careful than ever. Even if you got up, probably the formation would be a long way ahead and you would not be able to catch up. To be isolated in a dangerous place was as bad as being in the water. And then you would not know the road. There might be some of the enemy scattered about here. What could you do by yourself?

'Report! Could we flash a torch just once? It seems very dangerous in front of us,' somebody ventured to suggest to the sergeant.

'Good Heavens, no! Not by any means. This is a very dangerous spot, and it is more than probable that some remnants of the enemy are scattered here. Walk a bit slowly, if you like, but no flashlights!'

The atmosphere seemed to be very tense. When we heard that there might be scattered enemy near us we felt rather happy, because we were all eager to have a go at him. How nice it would be if in the complete darkness there should be a flash of gun-fire. It would be a lovely night scene.

Furthermore, there was this advantage in the dark night. You would not be able to know even if you were outnumbered by the enemy, and you would not be able to see the horrible sight of the wounded and the dead.

We became more brave and more sprightly. The night air was fresh, and when we reflected that we were fighting for truth, for humanity, for the oppressed people of the whole world, we felt more heroic than before. Then suddenly the thought came to me that if we had to fight, in the confusion at the time it was most probable that we could not distinguish who were our enemies and who were our own comrades, and we would be liable to kill our own people.

We soon passed the brook and reached the high mountain. The pass was through the middle of a field, and like two screens the mountain spread on either side of us.

'Bang! Bang! Bang!' We heard the distant report of guns.

'Halt!' shouted the lieutenant. 'If there are enemies in front of us, we divide into three formations, and the first formation in front must be ready to fire. But do not act in haste. Before I give a further order, do not fire.'

Every one of us was excited.

'Do not be afraid. I have told you there are the remnants of the scattered enemy whom we will encounter very soon. In the battle we should be very calm and brave, and not afraid of sacrifice.'

About three or four minutes passed, and the tense atmosphere was again relieved. We were walking slower than before, and as I was impatient of this slow marching, I tried to overtake some of the others.

'Why are you overtaking people? Do keep in order,' I was scolded by the sergeant.

'I want to walk in front, ready to fire,' I answered him heroically.

Splash! My right foot slipped and I fell in a pool of water. Luckily the water was not deep and I soon got out again.

'Hey, who fell down?' someone asked.

'It was I,' I answered, somewhat ashamed, and getting up hurriedly I followed the formation.

'You said you wanted to go in front, ready to fire, but you fell down instead. Be careful next time.' Somebody said this to tease me, and there was a general giggle. I, too, was inclined to laugh, but I did my best to suppress it.

We all thought that night marching was very interesting, and to some extent more comfortable; though there was no moonlight or starlight on that night, and we crept forward in the dark like blind men, it was cooler, especially when the gentle night breeze wafted towards us bringing the fragrance of flowers. The tree-tops as the wind passed over them made a gentle, melodious noise, which could be described as the most beautiful music in the world. I felt that it was intoxicating.

We continued walking on for many hours. Either we did not want to confess that we were tired, or we were so interested that we forgot that we had covered quite a long distance. Nobody complained about the march. Gradually, behind the distant mountain we saw some scarlet light. That was the dawn, and we were quite near to our objective. Soon it was broad daylight, and we began to want to break the night-long silence, for there was no point in being silent to avoid detection by our enemy any longer. I started to sing:

'Forward, comrades, dawn is before us. Forward, comrades!'

All the others joined in and we felt very happy.

Chapter XXV

DEMOBILISATION

EVERYTHING happened exactly as we had hoped. After a month and four days the war came to a sudden conclusion, and we came back to Wu Chang singing songs of victory. This West Punitive Expedition cost us more than seventy schoolmates and about a hundred comrades from the training troops. We captured many thousand rifles, and established the foundations of our Revolution in the heart of every citizen of that district. That was an unshakable monument for our cause. The greatest victory for us was that we had delivered from the hands of the military lords thousands and tens of thousands of oppressed people, who now would have a clear understanding of the Revolution and of our cause. We had sown the seeds of revolution in every place we passed. Victory! That was the final victory that we brought home.

One night, seven days after our return from the front, suddenly I heard the bugle. It was a moonless night, but there were a few sparkling stars in the sky. I was sitting with a group of women soldiers talking in the room of the head nurse, who was telling us her happy experiences during the expedition.

As we always did, within three minutes all of us were gathered in formation and had numbered off. We all looked at the five officers who were standing on the platform. They looked downcast, and we did not know what was the trouble. The lieutenant began:

'My schoolmates——' Strange, that was not his usual salutation to us. Even his voice was different. Before he went on any further we seemed to feel that he was trembling. We feared that something very unfortunate had happened, and sure enough he was proclaiming our unlucky fate. Indeed, he was reading out our sentence.

'First of all, I want you to be calm, to be brave, to be prepared for the worst.'

'What, are we going to the front again? But what is there to be afraid of?' That was in my thoughts.

'It is very unfortunate news I am going to tell you, but I want you not to be heart-broken. A revolutionary must be prepared for set-backs and obstacles. They are quite common. We should never give up and never be despairing.'

What was he going to say?

'Because the reactionary force is so great and because we want to preserve our revolutionary forces for a better time under better circumstances, and because the present conditions are pressing upon us, we have to demobilise for the time being.'

This was a thunderbolt from the blue, a bombshell in the night! It had almost knocked the life out of all of us. We were almost unconscious, but the lieutenant's voice went on heroically:

'Of course, this is not because we are afraid, not because we do not want to resist, for we are determined to have the final struggle. Those of you who are very robust and can run very fast may follow the Eleventh Army to fight. Otherwise you should all return to your own homes and suffer for the time being. In the very near future perhaps you will have a freer and happier life. Now each of you will receive ten silver dollars for your expenses, and I advise you to get some civilian clothes to disguise yourselves. The uniforms you must destroy.'

Heavens, what was this all about? Why should we be demobilised? Our hopes, our ideals, were they finished after such a short appearance.

After the lieutenant's report all the other four officers gave us some further advice, and their words made a very deep impression on our minds. One of them said:

'If you only hold your belief very firmly in your minds, if you can only think of revolution and sacrifice constantly, then, even if you cannot do anything at present, even if you have to stoop to compromise for a time, so long as you do not forget our great cause, you will eventually wipe out the military lords. All those who have been trained to be soldiers should be brave women and prepared to serve our cause in future.'

These words were sharp as knives piercing into our hearts, and many of us were shedding tears. So we were to leave the school to-morrow! To-morrow was the time when we should go into hell, for going back to our old-fashioned homes was as bad as going to hell. Alas, who wanted to go there?

During that whole night none of us went to bed. We stood on the training ground shouting slogans, singing and making speeches until daylight came. On the following day all the local girls went home in their beautiful dresses instead of in uniform, and I prepared to return to Changsha.

Because it would be easier for us to make them ourselves, I, Shu Yun, Shiang Shiao and San San bought some white linen to make Western frocks. I say Western frocks not because they were at all like the fashionable garments worn by European ladies, but just plain frocks without buttons, which were very easy to put on—you simply slipped them over your head.

Our hair had been cut very short, especially Shu Yun's, who had shaved her head, making it look very much like a bald pate, and because of that, no matter what masterly disguise she assumed, one could tell at a glance that she was a woman soldier and had carried a rifle. Then, too, we were all sun-tanned and our skins were very dark, and because we had been handling rifles for such a long period, our hands gave us away immediately.

'Our uniforms are gone, when shall we wear them again?' When I said this with a sigh and with tear-drops running down my face, Shu Yun could not suppress her loud sobs. When we looked at the new dresses we had just made, we were very much like mourners who were present at a funeral. We were silent, and very reluctant to change into them. We loved our uniform, and especially the leather belt, which we had rubbed so hard to make it shine. We really did not like to part with that. We remembered that when we had buckled it on the first time, we had thought it nonsense. It was hard and made our waist feel stiff and uncomfortable, so that when we were dismissed the first thing we did was to unbuckle the belt and give our waist a good exercising. Sometimes when we were in a hurry we forgot to buckle the belt as we went on to the drill ground, and because of that we had often been upbraided by our officers. By and by we got used to it, and except when we went to bed, we never left it off for a moment. We had fallen in love with that and our rifle, and, especially in winter time, the belt was a great help to us because it prevented the cold wind from piercing into our bodies. Our rifle, of course, was more dear to us than our lives. The destruction of the old system and the creation of a new society depended upon it.

But now everything was gone. Not only could we not take our rifle with us, but even the little leather belt had to be given up. Alas, alas!

This great, majestic women's army was now demobilised, but the spirit of the movement would live for ever. In 1927 the seeds of revolution had already been sown all over China. In every city and in every village I believed that in future the flowers of revolution would spring up, and final victory would certainly be ours!

Part Four

MY PRISON LIFE AT HOME

CHAPTER XXVI

MY HOME-COMING

WITH great reluctance we were at last obliged to change into our new dresses on the very afternoon when we had to leave Wu Chang—and we looked rather ridiculous in such queer garments. We looked at ourselves and each other and could not help laughing, and we decided that, as a last memento, we would go to a photographic studio and have our photographs taken. Our heads with short hair, or no hair at all, were very conspicuous with our so-called foreign dresses, so we decided to cover them with something. We went into a department store and bought four cheap straw hats, which were supposed to be of foreign fashion—but goodness knows what they looked like on us. Anyhow, they were very serviceable in the hot weather, and above all they were indispensable for covering our ridiculous heads.

Our departure from the station had a very sad atmosphere. A little more than a month ago, when we were leaving for the west of Hupeh, it was from this very station that we had been given such a grand send-off by thousands of well-wishers. It had been a dignified and also a magnificent affair. But to-day when we left Wu Chang for a second time it was a day of misery, with angry winds blowing fiercely and depressing clouds overhead. It seemed to us that on the faces of everybody in the station there was a look of sorrowfulness. Our hearts were very sad and there was only one thing which kept us going, and that was our firm belief that in future we would be masters of the world, and that upon our shoulders rested the salvation of the people. That was the only thought which kept us from throwing ourselves beneath the wheels on the iron rails.

At the first stop, police and soldiers rushed into the train to inspect every passenger. They wanted to know where we all came from, and made a thorough search of our luggage as well as of our persons. Of course, our appearance looked very suspicious, and we were questioned again and again. Fortunately we had a Mr. Li travelling with us, who was an aide-de-camp in the Army which had not been demobilised, and he took us under his protection. He told the soldiers that we were all relatives of his, and were students from a certain missionary school in Hankow who were going home for the summer holiday.

'Relatives? So many relatives? Perhaps they are the girls from the military school!' One of the policemen murmured this quite audibly to us, and Mr. Li looked at him very fiercely. However, the policeman went off without saying anything more.

When our train reached Yo Yang we had to go through more inspections and searches, but Mr. Li's uniform and Mr. Li's dignity preserved us.

When we arrived at Changsha, Mr. Li had to take leave of us, and our greatest problem was whether we could find lodgings. As soon as the *coup d'état* occurred in Wu Chang, none of the hotels were allowed to take visitors unless they were guaranteed by a responsible shop that they were not undesirable people. Also, we were not very rich, the combined wealth of us four girls being only six dollars. What could we do? I had to take my three comrades to impose upon the hospitality of my townswoman, Nan. She had been a schoolmate of mine in Da Tung, and we were very good friends. I knew that she would not turn us out, but as soon as her door closed behind us, she said tremblingly and in a whisper to me:

'Why on earth have you chosen such a time to come and see us? We are now in a world of terror. More people have been killed in the last few days than chickens and ducks. I could not take you for the night, because no house is allowed to take any visitors without having a signed guarantee by five other families. Every day policemen and soldiers come to inspect every house. As you come from Wu Chang it would be more dangerous than ever. . . .'

How could I blame her? In the eyes of others we must be more dangerous than the flood or beasts of prey. We certainly understood her difficulties, and if we had been in the same position we wondered if we would not do the same.

Shu Yun and San San started off on their home journey immediately. I and Shiang Shiao were obliged to go to the public hospital and stay there as patients. My feet were swollen and I really needed medical care. Shiang was to be my companion. Of course we had not the money for the hospital, but my townswoman, Nan, very kindly furnished me with five dollars. But five dollars went very easily in the hospital. Actually we were turned out of the hospital almost in the twinkling of an eye, and there was now nothing for us to do but to go home.

I had realised that at my home there would be more trouble than peace in store for me, but I had to go, even if it was just for the breaking-off of my engagement. By the time we reached Nan-Tien, which is not far from my village, it was about four o'clock in the morning. When I knocked at the door of the shop kept by my family, the keeper there thought it was my ghost that had come back. None of them then had the faintest hope that I was still alive. Half a month ago they had heard that I was actually at the front when I went out to fight, and after the news of the sudden political change in Wu Chang they knew that people like me would really have very little chance of survival.

Next morning we were given a sedan chair each, and very soon my old village gradually came in sight. As we drew near my heart began to sink, and I wondered whether the sedan chair bearers were feeling on their shoulders that their load was becoming heavier and heavier.

'Uncle Min, we shall be home very soon!' Shiang shouted excitedly from her sedan chair behind me. Shiang always called me uncle instead of aunt.

'Mm.' I was not so excited, and did not know what to say.

Passing the tea-shop, we came into a narrow lane, and within half a *li*, standing high up, was my home. It was a big new building which I had never seen before.

'This will be your prison!' I said this slowly to myself but I was not afraid. I had come home determined to fight it out. Although the prison was newly built, and must be very firmly built, I believed that with my will-power I could break away.

Home at last! My elder sister and my sister-in-law and many children came out to meet me, and of course there was my mother. Welcome was shining on all their faces, and I could see nothing but smiles. While the grown-ups held my hands very tightly, the children dragged me by my clothes, shouting, 'Do you know me, auntie?'

My mother had greatly aged since my departure. Her hair was all silver grey, and tears of joy ran from her eyes as she said:

'My child, you are much thinner than before. You must have suffered very much!'

While my mother wiped her tears, my elder sister and my sister-in-law also had reddened eyes, and my little niece, Yun Pao, who was only three, kept on asking me: 'Auntie, did you bring me a doll?'

In the middle hall I saw the space was crowded with new pieces of furniture, just varnished in bright colours of red and green and profusely decorated with gilt designs. I immediately knew that they were a part of my trousseau. I sighed, and was sorry for my mother, because she had been spending so much on me which would be completely wasted.

After lunch they took me to see the new house. It was of old-fashioned architecture, but the rooms were large, lofty and well lighted with windows, which at the same time gave plenty of air and lovely views of the beautiful country. According to what my mother said, she had originally intended to build two main buildings and two wings, but more than three thousand dollars had been spent on the main building, and because of financial difficulties she had had to give up the idea of the wings for the time being. The upper storey was not lofty enough to make living-rooms, because the windows were too small and there was not sufficient light. She also told me that the bricks, stone and wooden boards used for this new building were specially selected by herself, and would last a very long time.

I wondered if she was merely proud of the building, or whether she wanted me to know that it was too strong a prison for me to break. Indeed, if it had not been for the big guns of the Imperialists, I am sure it would be standing there after three thousand years. Anyhow, I was not much impressed by these magnificent buildings, because I had no wish to stay and die in this place. Even if they had built a house for me as good as the palace of the Pope in Rome, nothing would induce me to stay in it.

'Look how carefully your mother has been thinking of you. Over all this furniture, which is very richly varnished, I spent more than two months, scarcely having any sleep. On days when the wind blew I was afraid that the dust might rest on the newly gilt design and I had to get up during the night to cover them with oiled paper. In the daytime I was afraid the children would touch them or that they would be made dirty by the sparrows, and I had to keep looking at them scores of times a day. When the varnish workers were here I had to watch them all the time, to see that they were doing their work properly. Now, besides these forty pieces of beautifully varnished furniture, I have also prepared your coverlets, your mosquito nets, and other things. It is only for the making of your dresses that I have waited for your return.'

While my mother was proudly going on with this recital of her work I said not a word, but looked on the ground. She thought I was acting like an ordinary bashful girl who was naturally ashamed to say anything about her coming marriage, so she was happier than ever, and continued:

'I am sure this time it was the Goddess of Mercy who permitted you to come back! Ever since I heard that you had become a soldier I have been washing my face with tears, feeling that you would encounter dangers. I have burnt incense and offered numerous sacrifices for you in front of the Goddess of Mercy. When I heard that you had actually gone to the front I swooned three times, and one of those times I was unconscious for more than two hours. The people of the Shiao family were also worried about you, and sent many messages asking for tidings of you. Some of our neighbours thought that boy would not be lucky enough to have you for his wife. But now, thanks to heaven and thanks to earth, and thanks to the Goddess of Mercy, you have come back home safely.'

I had thousands of things to say to my mother, but I knew not how to begin. However, I decided that until my father came back I would say nothing about the breaking-off of my engagement. I knew my mother was a very obstinate woman, and to raise the subject with her would be just like pouring water on the back of a duck. It would be sheer waste of energy. So I kept silent for several days.

Chapter XXVII

MY QUARREL WITH MY MOTHER

ALTHOUGH there was no wireless in the country, news in my village travelled even quicker than the wireless. The Shiao family immediately knew that I had come back, and Chu Lin, my fiancé's uncle, wrote to us asking for a date to be fixed for the wedding. My eldest brother brought the letter to me, and said smilingly:

'What date shall I tell him in reply?'

'Better wait until father comes back.'

They answered the letter in accordance with my wish, but what would be the eventual outcome? Since the Shiao family knew that I had come back I could not possibly postpone the date of the wedding very much longer. If I did not break the engagement very soon it would be too late. Incidentally, my father came home that very night.

As soon as he read the letter from Chu Lin he summoned me to talk with him, and asked me what would be the best time for the wedding.

'I came home this time, specially for this, father.'

My father was evidently very much pleased, but I had to disappoint him.

'But you must remember what I wrote you last time. I said I could not possibly marry Shiao Kwang. Not only have we no love whatever for each other, but we simply do not know each other. I understand that his ideas and his interests are entirely different from mine, and besides, his personality, his ability and so on, I cannot understand. How could we become husband and wife?'

'What! Not marry him? You want to break off the engagement?' My father looked very angry.

'Yes, certainly, father,' I replied calmly and firmly.

My mother could not keep silent any longer and began to scold me by saying:

'Beast, beast!'

But I was not disturbed by it, and continued:

'Yes, the only purpose of my coming home this time was to break off my engagement with Shiao Kwang.'

'Ha, you want to break off your engagement, so you have come back? You have acted very unwisely. You should never have come back all your life! Since you have come back, there is no way of your getting out of it again. Marry you must, and I will see to that myself.' My mother was also very firm, and my father left me immediately in great fury.

I knew it would be no good to continue the discussion with my mother, and I retired to my bedroom to write a long letter, about five thousand words, giving my father all the reasons for my proposal to break off the marriage. I handed the letter to my father the next morning, and I was surprised to see that after he had read it he was not moved in the least, but began to upbraid me even more severely than before.

'As you say in your letter, the reasons for breaking off this engagement are chiefly these two: first, there is no love between you, and second, your ideas are different. Let me answer you very frankly. First, love can only be created between husband and wife after their marriage. To have love before they are married is ridiculous. As you have not yet married Kwang, how can you expect to have love for him? The second point is his ideas. Now that term can only be applied to revolutionary people, and has nothing to do with man and wife. Your marriage into the Shiao family is not a revolutionary affair, but is to fulfil your duty as a woman. The best you can do is to follow our ancient teaching, so that you can have a family in which "when the husband sings, the wife shall join in," to present descendants to the family and look after the cooking and all other domestic affairs of the house, and then you will become a good wife and a kind mother. Since this is not a revolutionary affair, what do you care about ideas?'

'Father, to have love only after the wedding is your philosophy of love. That was the special characteristic of the old-fashioned society, which is dead. Now, to have a happy union, men and women must know each other and must have agreeable feelings for each other first. After they first become known to each other they should become friends, and if their feeling for each other increases and becomes eventually love, then they can become companions for eternity, and that is what I think of marriage.

'As for their having the same ideas, that is even more important.

If two people of different ideas cannot possibly become friends, how can they become husband and wife who would share equal responsibility in building a happy life for eternity? People of different ideas would take different roads and have different careers, and they could not possibly hope to have any love for each other. Now, a marriage is a social affair rather than a private one. We are not merely wishing to establish a family and to raise children. The modern marriage is directly connected with the reforming of society. Those concerned should not only think of their own happiness but also of the good of society. As well as being husband and wife, they should also be good friends and trusting comrades. As Shiao Kwang's ideas are entirely different from mine, we haven't the slightest chance of being friends with each other and the fundamental condition of our marriage is gone.'

'M'm! Ideas? Why should women have such dangerous things? Why should women be allowed to join the Revolution? Since you have studied in the Normal School, after your marriage you can be allowed to be a school teacher in the local elementary school. That would be part of your contribution to society, as you said, and I am sure the Shiao family would not object to your doing that.'

'Please stop arguing with her,' my mother shouted to my father. 'This beast cannot be considered as a human being! Doesn't she realise that "father and mother are greater than heaven"? How dare she oppose our wishes? I sent you to school hoping you would learn propriety, righteousness, temperance and purity, but who would have thought that education would turn you into a beast without respect for your father and mother! Your marriage had been arranged by your father and mother when you were still at my breast. If you dare to oppose your marriage arrangements, it is as good as daring to oppose your father and mother. That would be a very shameful act indeed, and it would ruin our reputation and bring your ancestors into disgrace. I would rather die than allow you to do this.

"The water in Tung Ting Lake ripples forward,
  And happy husband and happy wife are destined by fate."

You should know this proverb, and realise that since you have been betrothed to him, marry him you must!

'Besides, the Shiao family is rich and has a very good reputation.

Shiao Kwang is a very good boy. He has no physical defects whatever; he is not blind, he is not maimed. What else do you ask for? Do you know that "a marriage may be arranged thousands of miles apart by a single piece of immortals' red thread?" Man and wife were arranged actually before their present existence. How dare you oppose the will of the immortals?'

When I heard these ridiculous quotations, I laughed hysterically and preferred not to waste my breath.

'In modern times, although I do not wish to force you, as the proverb says: "When you are married to a rooster you have to follow the rooster, and when you are married to a pig you follow the pig." I must say that Shiao Kwang is a very average man with whom you can find no fault. I saw his letter to your third elder brother and it was not altogether badly written. He can express himself all right.'

My father was more moderate, but his words made me laugh. His remark about the boy being able to write a tolerably readable letter was a great exaggeration. In reality he could not express himself at all. When he was in his elementary school I remember one of my teachers, who was also teaching him in his school, once said to me: 'Why are you and your future husband so different from each other? While you are standing at the top of the class in this school, he is always at the very bottom in his.' Later on I had many letters from Shiao Kwang, in which he had definitely proved that what my teacher had said about him was perfectly true. How could I possibly unite myself with such a worthless fellow?

My mother was still grumbling. She said that she regretted very much having sent me to school, the result of which had been that I had became a hopeless rebel. She said that henceforth she would never allow her grandchildren to go to school at all. When I heard this I was rather sorry for the children. Most of them were in their middle or elementary school days, and I knew from experience that my mother would never allow them to continue their studies. Alas! dear little children. How unfortunate they were to be suffering on account of my doings! Was I to blame for their misfortunes, or was society to blame?

'Schools are not much better than hell! Anybody who has been to school can act just like a devil. When they come home, no matter what happens they must break their matrimonial engagement carefully arranged by their parents,' my mother said aloud.

'Of course! What can parents know of the kind of husband or wife their children should have? Marriage is one of the most important things in one's life and should be left to the persons who are directly concerned. He or she would make a better choice than the parents.'

I knew that these words would not meet with approval, and that on the contrary I should be scolded for them, but my mind was going to burst if I did not air some of my views.

'Aren't you ashamed of yourself, you, an unmarried girl, to talk about selecting a husband! The Shiao family is a very respectable one. Your fiancé's third elder uncle was one of the representatives to the Provincial Assembly and also a very notable person in his district. All members of the family have been to school. Besides, the presents from their family to us have been very good, and that shows they know the rules of propriety. The year before last your fiancé came in person to congratulate me on my birthday. Now in return you want to commit this outrageous act against them. What face shall I have to see them again? You should remember the old proverb: "A good horse will not turn back to eat the grass behind him, and a good girl will never marry a second husband." '

Before my mother had finished her words my father put in:

'She would never read anything like that now. What girls of her type read nowadays are love stories in which girls commit suicide simply because they are not allowed to marry a young man of their own choice. Also stories in newspapers about girls breaking away from their homes because of their differences with their parents. Since they are influenced by these novels and newspaper stories, it is quite natural that we should have a girl who is dead set against her parents and the rules of propriety!'

'This is ridiculous! How can one set oneself against the rules of propriety?' my mother shouted in anger. 'They were established by our Sage, and for many thousands of years they have been governing our lives. How dare a mere girl like our daughter act against them? How can it be possible that with all pagodas and monuments erected in honour of chaste women of all ages, they cannot be a reminder to the girls of our generation? When we learn that a girl of twelve could determine to remain a widow when her future husband died, can it be possible that the modern girl would think of marrying twenty-four husbands in a year and still be without a husband when New Year's Day comes?'

I said nothing because I had now decided that to argue any further would be entirely useless. The only way was that I should be resolute in my struggle and never stop until the engagement was broken off.

'Although wealth and poverty are decided by heaven, human beings should take advantage whenever they can. The Shiao family is very rich, and if you would be a very good housekeeper and manage their estate wisely, you would become richer and richer, with plenty of rice fields and land, and have no end of happiness.'

My father tried to bribe me with promises of riches, and I felt it was an insult. If he thought that what I wanted was to have a happy, easy life, he did not understand me at all. He should have known that his daughter was a woman of character and not a snobbish girl who liked the rich and disdained the poor. I would rather marry a poor man who had nothing to bless himself with if we only had love for each other, and not in the least want to marry into a rich family.

My mother banged her hands on the table and said:

'What will you do if you are not going to marry him?'

It did not frighten me. I was only sorry for her, as the table was hard, and it must have been painful for her palms.

'She wants to break off the engagement,' my father answered for me, and I was grateful to him.

'What will she do if I do not allow her to break it off?'

'In her letter she says that she will die.'

'All right, let her die! I have brought her up, I have sent her to school, I have done everything for her. It must be that in my previous existence I owed her a great deal, so that in this present existence she is going to reclaim her . . . her. . . .' My mother burst into tears and cried aloud. She knocked her head on the wall, which did not frighten me, but my father ran to her and held her head in his arms.

My mother's cries brought my elder sister and sister-in-law rushing into the room to her rescue, and at this chance I darted out of the room and had a walk in the fields.

The sun was warm and the field was beautiful, but I had no heart for them.

A man in a white coat was approaching me from a distance. When he came near to me I perceived that it was my eldest brother. He asked me what trouble I was in, seeing that I was walking by myself, and I told him of the little comedy that I had just witnessed. After much hesitation he said with knitted brows:

'You should not have come back. Since you have come, how will you be able to get out of the fire again? I think . . . I think . . .'

'What are you thinking? Are you really thinking I will sacrifice myself to be married to that worthless Shiao Kwang?'

'I . . . I . . . Yes, that is what I am thinking.'

'No! I will never marry him. I must fight to the last!'

'Our mother is a more terrible person than any famous tyrant in the histories, ancient or modern, Chinese or foreign. Do not you know that already? Because I took your sister-in-law to Yi Yang without getting her consent, I was condemned by her as one who would oblige his wife by disobeying his parents, and was made to kneel down for more than two hours with a big basin of water balanced on my head. That is a thing which no one should forget. Besides, the marriages of your second and third elder brothers and your elder sister were arranged by her, and they are all suffering and miserable, but none of them dares to breathe a word about divorce. Although you are braver than any of us, I think your bravery would be much better applied on the battle-field than at home. We cannot possibly have a Revolution in our own house!'

This last remark by my eldest brother was meant to be friendly, but I was not amused.

'My eldest brother, please do not be sarcastic, and please do not think that I am powerless at home. To tell you frankly, I knew that the moment I got back I should lose my freedom. But I thought that if I did not come home to break off the engagement I should not have a clear conscience to contract a marriage with anyone else. The Shiao family would be in a position to discredit my marriage for the reason that my first betrothal was not broken off. In order to avoid future troubles I decided to come back and fight the old system with its own weapons and on its own ground, and I have the firm resolution that until my aim is achieved I will never stop. I had rather sacrifice my life in this fight than surrender to the dark old system. . . .'

'I had better hurry home at once in case mother knows that

I am talking here with you, and may think that I am conspiring against her.'

My poor eldest brother! He was entirely controlled by mother. He dared not listen to me any longer and was glancing furtively here and there to make sure that we were not seen.

'All right, you had better hurry home. I do not want to compromise you or anybody.'

'All right, I hope you will succeed!' He was still sarcastic, and with a broad smile he went away. I stayed in the field for quite a long time before I returned.

I did not take any breakfast because I did not want to see my father's and mother's faces, which would take away anybody's appetite. When evening came, I went to bed. My elder sister, my eldest sister-in-law and my third sister-in-law saw that I had no supper, and knew what was in my mind. They came to comfort me, but dare not say anything because my mother was in the next room, and every single word or movement in my room could be distinctly heard by her. All they could say to comfort me was to ask me not to be sorrowful, and as their words were really meaningless I hoped that they would never come to my room again. My aunt—my mother's younger sister—was invited by my sister to stay with us in order to pacify the family quarrel. Her husband was working at the educational bureau and was only earning a wage of six dollars a month. Their two boys were serving in the Army, the younger one being a sergeant and the other one was once a vice-lieutenant, but because he was too deeply versed in the bad habits of the Army—gambling and prostitution—he was dismissed from the Army and his whereabouts were unknown. My aunt had three boys and one girl. The youngest boy had died two years ago, and being a very clever boy my aunt mourned his loss so much that she had now become blind.

She was an absolute fatalist who held that everything had been predestined in a previous existence. She believed in gods, and every day she read the Buddhist scriptures. She was also a vegetarian and even more superstitious than my mother. But otherwise she was much more open-minded than my mother, because she allowed her sons to marry from their own choice. Her daughter, who also died at the age of ten, had not been betrothed by her to anybody. She even advised my mother:

'Now the world is changing, you must not be too strict with

your children. They are all well-educated people and they have their careers before them, and you must not restrict them too much.'

But my mother not only refused to listen to her advice, but also scolded her as not being qualified to be the head of a family. My mother said:

'No matter how much the world has been changed, parents are always parents and children are always children. If I am not able to restrict the actions of my children, how can I be the head of the family?'

Although my aunt had her own ideas, she was not in a position to quarrel with my mother. When she came to my room to see me, she dared not say anything until she heard that my mother had gone out of her room.

'Min Kon, you must not quarrel with your mother. You know that she has a very bad temper, and you should try your best to humour her. You know that our marriage is predestined in our previous existence. Although your future husband is not as clever as you are, you should overlook that and condescend a little bit. Then everybody will say that you sacrificed yourself for the good of all and you will be remembered by your descendants.'

'My aunt, please do not say such things to me. You do not seem to understand my troubles, so do not try to comfort me. That will only annoy my mother. The best thing to do is to pay no attention to me.'

My tears rushed down my cheeks like a torrent, and my kind aunt could not find any words to say and she also shed tears.

Chapter XXVIII

CONFINED BY MY MOTHER

From now onwards my life had some resemblance to that of a prisoner.

Night came ; quiet, calm, dark and endless night.

In the country after eight o'clock everything was quiet, but at my house there seemed to be whisperings going on long after the usual bedtime, and I always imagined they were talking about me. It was never before midnight that I could get to sleep.

The moon shone in the middle of the sky with her gentle rays reflected on my mosquito net, and one or two mosquitoes made tiny incessant buzzing sounds which made me restless.

Tossing in my bed, I began to think that I would have no end of trouble with my parents. I had no hope that the matter could be settled peacefully. Since my parents had decided to act contrary to my wishes and since I could not surrender to them, there was no possibility of compromise. Indeed, they so firmly believed in their authority over me that they were ardent supporters of the rule prevailing in the old society saying that 'when a father wants his son to die, then die he must.' It happened that I was a stout rebel from the old society and my ideas were at least three genera- tions ahead of those of my parents. How could it be possible that we should not quarrel? However, I was determined to fight for final victory.

But I was fighting against overwhelming odds. In that place there was not a single person who could really understand me, sympathise with me or fight at my side, except Shiang, who had been my schoolmate throughout my elementary days, my middle school days and the military and political school. According to our relationship, she was a generation younger than I and con- sequently she always called me her 'uncle' because I hated the term 'aunt.' My sister often shed tears in sympathy with me but she was helpless. She herself was suffering from an unhappy marriage from which she could not free herself, so how could she do anything to help me? Indeed, as she had been suffering for so long, there seemed to her no reason why I should not suffer like herself. Why should a girl leave her family to study abroad and marry somebody of her own choice? Her tears were simply tokens of her love for me and also expression of her own trouble, but nothing more. She also knew that I might do something desperate, because in my younger days, when I was so bent on studying and could not get what I wanted, I once tried to starve myself to death. She knew I was very obstinate and would never give in. Although she seemed to realise what I was prepared to do, she nevertheless gave me no assistance in escaping from this pit of fire. All the tears she shed over me were wasted. What is the use of tears when it comes to a life and death struggle?

As for Shiang, although she was only a very short distance from me, she was not allowed to come and see me. Her family was one exactly like mine, treating their offspring with tyranny because she would not marry her fiancé—who was a gambler as well as a debauchee—so she too was imprisoned at home. Even if she could have obtained permission to come and see me we would not have been able to have any heart-to-heart talks, for my mother would certainly be at our side.

As for my eldest brother, he was a coward who was so afraid of my mother that now he had acquired a lot of her ideas. He might be in sympathy with me, but I did not know what he would say in front of my mother. At any rate, I could not see eye to eye with him, and it seemed unlikely that he could give me any help.

My third elder brother was far away in Changsha at present. He would have been very helpful, but as our old saying goes: 'Distant water cannot put out a near-by fire.' All he could do would be to write letters to father and mother pleading for me, but what good would those letters do? On the contrary, would they not increase their anger against me?

I had to fight alone, without any help, and without much hope. In spite of that I would never surrender.

To commit suicide was perhaps the only solution. To suffer physically for a short moment and to end my troubles and worries of a lifetime! What is the meaning of life? Human beings are mortal. No matter what great and magnificent things one may achieve, when the moment came for one to breathe one's last, everything would be gone. The world is a mirage and all the things in it are ephemeral. Rather than allow my life to be spoiled by others I preferred to sacrifice it myself. After all, my life was my own; I had the right to continue or discontinue it. Perhaps death was my eventual peace and my final victory.

It seemed to me at that time that apart from death I could not find another way out. At first I had thought my letter to my father would gain his sympathy, for I firmly believed that every word in that letter was written as with my tears, and that my sincerity would move anybody. But now everything clearly indicated that my father was entirely on the side of my mother. His firm and cold attitude towards me now made it difficult for me to believe that he was the man who had wrapped me up in his fur coat and patted me tenderly when I was a little girl. I began to think that feelings were very selfish things. If your children were obedient to you, then your feelings towards them were tender, but once their interests were against yours, then you began to consider them not as your children but to act merely to promote your own interest. I shuddered at that thought.

As to personal feelings, I began to realise that these were things which could not be understood. I had always thought that a mother's feelings for her child were above all things on the earth, and now that I realised that such a philosophy was all wrong, my heart was broken. My mother, who had loved me, now loved nobody but herself. What was there to live for?

The dim moonlight was beginning to fade and the barking of the dogs could be heard in the distance. The roosters at my house began to sing their morning song, but my room was still horribly dark. Dawn was beginning to break in the east, and I could hear that my mother was discussing something with my father. Though I tried to listen, I could overhear nothing.

Death! Was there nothing else for me but death? Why should I not think of my future, my ambition? I had often blamed those people who committed suicide as being cowardly. To strive for life is an instinct of human beings, and why should I seek death? Even if I am as small as a grain of sand in the big sea of society, and my death would not really affect it at all, that would not be any excuse for my cowardice. And there is one's own conscience; how could I face my conscience when I realised that I was trying to avoid my own duty to society? After all, I had been enjoying the benefits of society by being fed, clothed and educated. Furthermore, I should remember that I had been baptised in revolution and was given the responsibility of reforming society; I had been made a warrior and privileged to fight on the battle-field. I had taken a solemn vow to struggle until the emancipation of 1,250,000,000 oppressed human beings had been achieved. I had proclaimed that I was not one of those cowardly ordinary girls, but a courageous, determined and full-blooded person. My duty was to fight against the unreasonable old system. How could I suddenly forget all my duties? To die would mean that I was defeated and that the old system had won. The old-fashioned society was a devil, and had massacred numerous people, and it was still opening wide its bloody mouth intending to swallow all the young people who had not sufficient courage. Furthermore, I should realise that to commit suicide would be a very unwise thing. It would mean that a rebel from the old society had been wiped out and had saved them a bullet. Even if one had not the courage to kill other people, one should at least do something towards revolution. To be killed was better than to commit suicide.

These conflicting ideas of life and death struggled in my thoughts for a very long time, and at last life succeeded. I remembered that my eldest brother was going to the city, and as a last forlorn hope I wrote a very long letter asking him to see whether he could arrange to get any help for me in the city.

When an opportunity arose I secretly handed the letter to my eldest brother, who, after glancing over it, began to shake his head, which indicated that he could not help me at all. We said nothing to each other, but shed tears in silence.

I began to suffer from sleeplessness. When the night was far advanced I would open my windows and let in the breeze. In the moonlight which shone on my bed I examined my feet, which were swollen and very painful. I sobbed all night, but I never heard a word from my mother in the next room. Alas, I was now really an abandoned child and could never hope for my mother to comfort me, never hope to feel her warm, tender arms, and never hear her voice saying, 'My heart, my treasure!' I remembered that in my younger days when I had any ailment she would spend all her days and nights with me looking after me, and now if I died in my bed I do not think she would come and look at me. My heavens! what was the matter with us? My tears glistened in the moonlight when they fell on my pillow. I wished that the moon, which was also shining on my mother, would convey some of my thoughts to her. Why should she be so cruel and cold towards me?

When my eldest brother went to the city I still hoped that he would write to me telling me that I could get away. I waited, and five days went by, ten days, a month, and still no letter from him. At last all hopes of help from him were gone. I must help myself.

Shiang's younger sister, Chin Chin, was a very lively girl of twelve years of age, and she performed many good services between us which we would never forget. She was the only means of communication between us.

At that time I was no better than a prisoner, spending all my days and nights in that room of mine. In the daytime my only companion was a sunbeam coming through the window, and at night my sole visitor was the moonlight coming in the same way. No outside visitors were allowed to see me, and I was confined in this solitude for a long time.

One day my father suddenly called me out of my prison. It was Chin Chin who had come to see me. I was greatly relieved at the sight of her, and words failed to describe my joy.

'How is your sister?'

'She is very well, much better than you are.'

When my mother was not looking at her she secretly passed me a little note, crumpled into a tiny ball. We did not say much to each other, and I soon went to my room with the secret note, which contained only these words:

'This is unbearable. We must prepare to escape.'

That was obviously the only way, and I was so glad I now had a comrade in arms.

My father seemed to be a changed man now, and he regarded me as his enemy. He would not say a word to me, but he had his smiles for the children. This made me think he was now a man of stone. My mother was, of course, much worse. From her appearance it seemed as if she could devour people alive. In my presence she never looked at me, but when she was speaking to others she was very amiable and full of smiles, and she had the hypocrisy to tell them that I was such a nice and dutiful girl that I was actually preparing my own wedding dress.

'A girl brought up in a proper way and in a good family is entirely different. Although your daughter has been to school in the cities, she has not become a dreadful "free" girl. You, madam, are indeed a very fortunate mother.'

I heard people compliment my mother in this fashion, and I shuddered at the words. But my mother had the audacity to reply:

'While other people's girls become rebels once they are allowed to study outside, my daughter would never think of doing any-thing of that kind. You know, she is such a good girl that even if she became the Empress in Peking, she would still be my obedient daughter.'

I really do not know whether she was pretending, or whether she believed I would yield to her eventually. Anyhow, she kept watch on me very carefully and I was not allowed any freedom. While my feet were swollen as if they were two big pillows, I was not allowed even to see a doctor. I did not blame myself for joining the Army, for my malady was entirely due to my camping in the open. They gave me some ointment, but that was no remedy.

My sister one day told me that all my letters had been destroyed by my father, and this was such a shock to me that I swooned. Alas, many a sleepless night I had spent writing to my friends, and it seemed that none of them, except the one I passed to my elder brother, could have reached any of them. When I came to, I cried and cried.

'Please do not cry, my younger sister. Even if you cry yourself to death, they will not allow you to write to others.'

My sister's words sobered me, and I stopped crying. Since they used these unfair means against me, I must use the same means towards them. I immediately planned to escape, and I looked for a chance to discuss it with Shiang. As she was still not allowed to see me, nor was I allowed to see her, we must bide our time.

For a whole month I received no letters, and was not allowed to read any newspapers. I knew that even if there were any letters they would be in my father's hands. One day when there was no one about, I went to my father's room, and found under his pillow a letter from Mr. Sun Fu Yuan, saying that he enclosed a postal order for twenty dollars, for my travelling expenses to Hankow, but the postal order was not to be found.

I was not only forbidden to read either books or newspapers, but neither was I allowed to write, for no paper was given to me. The only paper on which I could lay my hands was lavatory paper.

On that evening I decided to write to Mr. Sun, and to trust Chin Chin with the letter. As it was impossible for me to write in my room, which was carefully kept under observation by my mother, I had to write it in the lavatory. Because I spent a slightly longer time there than usual, my mother immediately broke open the door of the lavatory, and finding I was writing, she said:

'What! you are so clever as to invent this very ingenious plan? Hand the letter to me immediately.'

I was so furious that I threw everything into the water.

After this incident we became deadly enemies, and I was observed even more strictly than before.

Chapter XXIX

MY PILGRIMAGE

WHEN my mother saw that my feet were still unwell, she said that because at my birth a promise had been made to the god of the Holy South Mountain for a pilgrimage to be made, and that promise had not been kept, so I was being punished by the god. She therefore stated that on the 28th of the 8th month we must make the pilgrimage to the Great South Mountain. On the preceding night, after my bath, I was ordered to put on a new set of underclothes. Next morning my mother dressed me in a suit of red jacket and trousers and a red turban, which she had specially made for me for this purpose. I looked in the mirror and was shocked to see that I had now become a red devil.

From my early days I had objected to this senseless superstition, but why was it that to-day I was as tame as a gentle lamb, placing myself entirely at my mother's disposal? There were the following reasons: firstly, I had been confined in one room for such a long time that I was longing for a breath of fresh air. I believed the trip would do good to my health. Secondly, the Great South Mountain is one of the famous five mountains of China, with lovely views, and I was thinking of availing myself of this opportunity to visit this beautiful place. Last, but not least, I was hoping for a chance to make my escape during the journey, and that if I succeeded I would indeed tender my sincere thanks to heaven and earth and the god of the Great South Mountain.

From my home to the mountain was a journey of more than five hundred *li*. Even if we did not waste half a minute on our way, it would mean that we had to travel ten days in sedan chairs to get there and come back. My mother told me that, from the day we started until the day we got back, the whole family would go on a vegetable diet, and at our departure everybody must kneel down in the courtyard and knock their heads on the ground. More ridiculous still was that everybody would cast two pieces of bamboo on the ground in order to get the right augury for permission to have our farewell meal. Should the right augury not appear, they would continue to cast those pieces of bamboo and never dare to get up. When I asked if, in the case of such an augury never turning up, we were going to starve to death, my mother answered promptly that sincerity would certainly move heaven and earth and the gods.

In addition my mother taught me to sing the song of the pilgrimage, which began thus:

'The Holy God of the South Mountain
Was the Heavenly Lord who looked after country and people.
Sincere pilgrims want to return gratitude to their parents;
They have come to kneel down and burn incense.
They pray that their parents will live for a thousand years,
And that happiness and health will be granted to them.
. . . . . .'

This song had to be learnt by heart, and should be repeated all the time, either when we were in the sedan chairs or when we were resting in hotels. However, as I was only allowed to do this in a whisper, I did not care much about it, and just pretended to murmur it, though actually I was not saying the right words at all.

One day, when my sedan chair bearers were some distance from my mother, I started a conversation with them, one of whom told me this story about the mountain:

'The Holy God is as good as alive. One day there was a lady pilgrim who came to kneel after every five steps that she took, and a passer-by who saw that she had lovely small feet ventured to touch her foot with his hand. Lo and behold, the man was as if struck by lightning and could not take his hand back. His fingers continued to stretch out, and he was laughed at by everybody.'

'Yes, that was true,' rejoined the other chair bearer. 'Another time I saw a man who came to pay a fasting pilgrimage. He had not taken anything for eight days and was consequently very hungry. When he came to a peach tree he looked around, and as he could not see me because I was hiding behind a tree, he thought to get one of the peaches. But as soon as his hand touched the fruit he was as if struck by lightning, and became sick. His eyes rolled upwards and he was dead within ten minutes. When the people later on saw the dead man on the road, they realised that the gods, although invisible to us, were never more than three feet away.'

'Have you really seen these things yourselves?'

'Y—yes,' they answered hesitantly. But I knew they were lying.

'Better not talk nonsense. If you really believe in the gods, you must not make up stories even if they are in favour of the gods.'

Although my mother's sedan chair might be a little behind mine when we were on the road in daytime, she always kept close watch upon me at night. When we put up at a small inn, she would confine me to my room and never allow me to go out again. On the third night of our journey we came to a place called Shi Cha Wan, and we stayed the night at an inn surrounded by an extensive bamboo grove. A bend of the river passed the building, and on either side of the water there were lovely tall pine trees. Indeed, the whole place presented such a lovely scene that it made me feel poetical. As I was having a walk in the courtyard of the building, looking at the scenery in the distance, a young girl of about seventeen or eighteen came in. She had seen my red dress and knew that I was a pilgrim. She approached me with a smile and I invited her to sit down in the courtyard.

'Are you paying a pilgrimage to the Great South Mountain?'

'Yes.'

'Have you been to school?'

'N-n-no,' I replied, hesitantly.

'That is strange. Appearances are against you.'

'I am speaking the truth. I cannot read or write.'

As though she were a fortune-teller, she examined me from head to foot very carefully and made me feel guilty.

Fortunately my mother was at that time kneeling before the shrine of the god in the inn, and she took no notice of me.

'More than two months ago we had a Women's League here which was established for the emancipation of the oppressed women in this locality. All the girls who were members had to unbind their feet, cut their hair and not worship any gods.'

Evidently she was a girl with new ideas. I was very pleased to meet her and asked her about the things which had happened here before the Revolution was suppressed. When I saw that my mother was entirely devoted to her act of worship, I stole away with this

6

young girl to her house and we talked for about half an hour. Her mother was also a very open-minded person. Neither did she believe in the gods, and she gave me two salted eggs which I received and ate heartily.

Soon my mother rushed into this house, and in spite of being before strangers, she scolded me very severely and dragged me back to the inn. She made me kneel down before the shrine immediately and said:

'The innkeeper's wife told me that the young girl was a wretched woman who was once a member of the Women's League, and who talked a lot of nonsense such as freedom in love. Why should you talk with her?'

I maintained silence.

'Surely you have not drunk any tea in this strange house? You know that in our process of pilgrimage we must not taste anything from strangers, not even a drop of water.'

'No, I have not drunk their water.' But in my mind I said, 'Although I have not drunk a drop of their water, I have eaten two salted eggs which I very much enjoyed.'

When I was made to kneel down beside her and ask for forgiveness from the gods, I was really recollecting what the girl had told me:

'The Women's League was disbanded about two months ago. That could not be helped, but we are not in despair. We hope that the day will come when we will be free. If the women do not join in the Revolution, they will never be free again. . . .'

After sitting in a sedan chair for five whole days all my bones ached. Although in the morning and at twilight the landscape on the way was always intoxicating, I could not enjoy it very much, and when the red disc of the sun came up early in the morning, shooting a thousand golden rays across the world, it never gave me high spirits. I ought to have realised that life is like a conflagration, full of heat and power, and of light! I should discard my worries and troubles, and my heart should really be filled with warmth from the sun, and I should have courage to face any adversity. Above all, I should be as happy as an angel, forgetting my temporary restrictions. In these beautiful surroundings one should have unlimited hope.

But when one looked back, one realised that time was passing very rapidly, and that before one could form any plans for the future, one had already been fettered by the past, which brought remorse and despair.

The evening was comparable to the last days of a man; in fact, it was somewhat like the time when a man was ready to be put in his coffin. Everything was gone, all hope had disappeared. Like the floating clouds in the sky, it had been swept away by the breeze. Even the most brilliant coloured clouds and lovely evening haze would only be there for a few seconds, to be wrapped in complete darkness before one could enjoy its existence long. In my moments of sorrowfulness I liked to look at the evening sun, for it foretold that the darkness of the night was soon approaching, and I felt 'let the worst come to the worst, and let the whole world be kept in darkness for ever!' However, these depressed thoughts were only temporary, and very soon I would be hoping that the morning would come, and that in the light of the sun everything would be alive, bright and warm again.

At last we arrived in the district of the South Mountain. Though it is a small city, not to be compared with Changsha, the capital, it has a magnificent temple, which is almost like a palace. Pilgrims crowded the place, and I was told that it was busy all the year round. Everyone seemed to be busy there, and never spent more than a few hours in the place, for directly they had made their offerings in the temple they would hurry on to the top of the Chu Yun Peak to finish the pilgrimage.

From the foot of the mountain to the peak, the journey there and back is about sixty *li*. One has to start very early in the morning, and by the time one returned it would be almost nightfall. The road up was as difficult as a step-ladder, except that it was zig-zag instead of straight. Sedan chairs cannot be used, and one had to climb on foot very slowly. The sedan chair bearers acted as porters to carry our incense sticks and paper money.

Perhaps I had a somewhat better time when I was travelling than when confined at home. My feet were not so painful as before. Especially when we were climbing up I was very quick in my movements and soon left my mother a long way behind. Once I looked back at her and I saw that she was standing still and was murmuring her song of pilgrimage. I then perceived that she was trembling as if she had some malady. I ran back to her and asked her to sit down and rest a little before she proceeded. To my great surprise she suddenly knelt down and said:

'My holy god, please forgive her, she is an ignorant girl who does not know what she says. Please, my holy god, be very merciful and pardon her.'

'Why, what offence have I committed? Why should you say this?'

'No matter how difficult it may be for me, I must not rest. If you are sincere enough, the gods will send you up with a breath of wind.'

'All right, you wait here until the breath of wind sends you up.'

That remark was indeed a serious offence. My mother immediately ordered me to kneel down, and I was kept there for several minutes, and of course she had to say her prayers frequently before we started again.

On the road there were several places where you could find food pavilions, where tea, water, potatoes and Indian corn were sold. I asked my mother to stop for a while for us to look at the beautiful view behind us, and also to have a rest and buy something to eat, but she always severely upbraided me and ordered me to continue my journey. When we were quite near to a place called the Gate of the South Heaven, my mother suddenly had an attack of stomach-ache and could not move a step. She called the sedan chair bearers to bring me back, and ordered me to kneel down for fresh prayers.

'What is the trouble now?'

'You must kneel down immediately. I cannot move a step now. It must be that you have offended the gods again.'

'That is ridiculous! If I have offended the gods they should punish me, not you!'

'Not another word! Kneel down immediately.'

There was no other way for it but to obey her and kneel down. After a few minutes of rest in this rather uncomfortable position we were somewhat refreshed and were able to proceed again, but my obstinate mother would say to the sedan chair bearers:

'The holy god is truly alive. You see, as soon as this naughty child knelt down to offer prayers, my malady went immediately, and we were able to proceed again at once.'

I told her very frankly that the holy god was none other than herself, and that her stomach-ache and her panting were caused because she wanted rest. After she had knelt down for a few minutes naturally she felt better and was able to proceed again. However, my candid opinion was condemned as another offence, and we had another rest before we climbed up again.

Passing through the Gate of the South Heaven, we came to the Cliff of Lions, the Temple of Pines, and soon we arrived at the Palace of the God of Fire, which is not very far from the Peak of Chu Yun, which is the name of the god of fire. This palace is a very extensive building, and it was crowded with pilgrims, some dressed like myself completely in red, while others were fasting pilgrims who had almost starved themselves to death and looked like skeletons. There were also kneeling pilgrims who kept on murmuring:

'My first kneeling was to the God of Heaven and of the Sun and Moon.

'My second kneeling was to the God of Earth and the Universe.'

The palace was full of smoke and incense, and the sounds of the bell and drum and the 'wooden-fish' and other instruments. In fact, everyone in the building was acting like people possessed by a devil, kneeling anywhere they could find room and murmuring strange things. Suddenly it came to my mind that this was a picture of hell, and the pilgrims, having suffered many days of difficulty on their way here, gave a very realistic impression of what devils would look like.

While I was looking at these people and thinking these things, I was suddenly directed by my mother to kneel down again because the so-called god would not consent to receive my offerings—as explained by my mother. I had to cast the two pieces of bamboo more than thirty times before I could obtain the right augury. My mother urged me to knock my head on the ground repeatedly, and while I was doing so I could not help counting how many times the lady who knelt next to me had knocked her head. Before I left her she had knocked more than sixty times, and was still doing so.

I thought that directly we had offered my worship there would be an opportunity for me to have a look around at the lovely view from the peak of the mountain, but unfortunately my mother was in a great hurry. After we had made our way up and had reached the top, we were not allowed to stop a second before making our way down again.

Defeated! My scheme was utterly defeated. Not only had we

no time to enjoy the landscape, but also the slightest chance of getting away from my mother was denied to me. There was nothing for it but to follow her and go home in despair. That famous mountain gave me no other impression on my first visit than that I realised it was very high and that the path upwards was very steep. Although I did not enjoy my trip there, I had seen numerous ridiculous sights and foolish acts by human beings. If that was not helpful towards my future in any other way, it at least contributed something towards my education.

CHAPTER XXX

BAD NEWS

IN the afternoon of a rainy day we had a letter from my third elder brother. Before the letter was read my heart went pit-a-pat as if in anticipation of bad news. The augury was right. The letter told us in a few words that my second elder brother had died in Nanking.

My heavens, it was only a week ago that we had heard from him, and now he was no more!

I felt at that time as if I had lost my soul. I lost my interest in life and my courage for struggle. While lamenting over the death of my second elder brother, I wished I could follow him to the Yellow Springs of the other world.

Although we were five brothers and sisters, I loved my second elder brother best. When I was studying in the elementary school he sent me story books and wrote me many interesting letters. Then when I entered the Girls' Normal School, he did his best to put me on the road to literary study. At that time he was teaching in the Chin San Middle School in Shansi province and his salary was not a very big one, but nevertheless he always sent me twenty or thirty dollars a year, especially for me to buy books. After his return to Changsha he gave me many famous books, and if there was anything which I could not understand he would very kindly explain it to me.

In the spring of 1926 he contracted consumption, and spat quite a lot of blood. After he had been treated at the Yale-in-China Hospital he was sent to the Kwan-Tao Pavilion in the Yo Lu Mountain for convalescence. I gave up my school for the time being and spent more than four months with him. He could take nothing except a little milk and chicken soup, and I spent all my time in looking after him, recording his temperature and his pulse. At night I would stay by his bedside and sing lullabies of our childhood days to make him sleep, and would tell him stories of my schooldays to amuse him. Once I went across the river to get something for him to eat, and as I was not back in three hours he was so worried about me that he spat blood again. On my return he took hold of my hand and said, with tears in his eyes:

'My good younger sister, please do not leave me any more. I had rather not eat these nice things you brought me than miss you for so long.'

My third elder brother at that time was a teacher in Yo Yuen Middle School, and he could only manage to come and see my second elder brother on Sundays. So during the week-days, besides a boy who did some rough work and cooking for us, we two, brother and sister, were solitary companions in that lonely mountain place.

I remember on one early summer night, when the moon was shedding her mercury light on the good earth and the evening breeze was blowing gently among the trees, making a sweet sound, and the insects were chirruping all around us, we thought that the whole Yo Lu Mountain was like a beautiful maiden taking a bath in the green moonlight. The little boy was already asleep, and my second elder brother wanted me to support him so that we could have a walk outside in the moonlight. I was afraid that the walk would excite him too much and would probably make him spit blood again, but my dissuasion was not successful, and I had to take hold of him as we went out of the house. The moment he was out of doors he exclaimed:

'Ah, lovely, lovely! The moonbeams are like the water, and the water is like the sky.'

I was so happy that I did not realise what he was saying, but he laughed and said:

'Look, my younger sister, after being confined to bed for so long I was not able to compose even a single line of poetry.'

I supported him back and he lay down in his chair.

The gentle breeze blew away not only the heat, but also my second elder brother's sickness. He was very happy and he told me about the beautiful scenery in the moonlight that he saw in Chefoo.

'The mystery of the sea, especially the beautiful sea in the moonlight, is something beyond your comprehension. If I am better by the summer vacation I will take you to either Chefoo or to Tsing-Tao to see the sea.'

Because of the careful treatment he underwent, he became better every day. Unfortunately another calamity fell upon him.

He fell in love with a very good friend, Miss Shu. At first their love was mutual, but in less than three months Miss Shu suddenly gave up my second elder brother and married another man. After this unfortunate incident my second elder brother left Changsha immediately and became secretary to the Fourth Army in Wu Chang. His life in the Army was nothing but hardship. A camp-bed, an army blanket and a few books to serve as pillow were all he had at his camp.

While I was undergoing my training in the Military School he came to see me every week, giving me candies, smoked fish and stewed beef.

'My second elder brother, next time you come you must bring me more beef and fish. I have so many friends here who enjoy them. If you don't, they will not allow me to see you.'

Of course, I was only teasing him, but he took it very seriously, and the next time he came he brought with him six big parcels of food, melon seeds, and salted shrimps, besides his usual present. They were things we liked, and we had a very big party. While we were enjoying ourselves we heard the sound of the bugle, and had to leave our repast unfinished to go out and get into formation on the training ground. He waited for us for two hours before he left, and when we went back to the drawing-room again after the meeting we were disappointed to find that both my brother and all the refreshments had disappeared. At first we thought it was my brother who had tried to annoy us by taking the things away, but later on the officer on duty told us that he had the room cleaned because the place was so dirty.

In June he set out for Honan. He did not tell me he was leaving, but he wrote a letter to me in which he said:

'My dearest younger sister, do not worry about my going. In the very near future we shall be holding each other's hand on the battle-field.'

A few days afterwards I also set out for the west of Hupeh, and since then we had been separated beyond any chance of meeting again, and no news passed between us. When I arrived home I made many enquiries but did not know where he was until a few days ago, when we heard that he was again spitting blood, and now this tragic news suddenly came upon us.

I cannot possibly write anything further. The death of my second elder brother is one of the most heart-breaking pages in

6 *

the history of my life. Very sorrowful impressions were marked on my heart. Like a person who has lost his soul I cried all day, 'My second elder brother! my second elder brother!' Sometimes I cried and sometimes I laughed, and people began to say that I was crazy.

I considered that the death of my second elder brother was caused by the bad influence of the old society. I wanted to wipe away the old system in revenge. At night I blew out my lamp and waited calmly, silently for the return of his ghost.

But one night, two nights, ten nights went by. I spent all the time shedding tears and heaving big sighs, but his ghost never came back to me.

I spat a lot of hot red blood, and I began to think that I might follow in the footsteps of my second elder brother. I might then be turned into a little bird, so that I could fly with my second elder brother to Tsing-Tao, to Chefoo, or even across the Himalayas to the end of the world, to some very lonely island in the ocean, or some beautiful forest in an unknown land, to the border of the heavens, to the spaces where we could be free!

The news of the death of my second elder brother was a hard blow to everybody. My father was heart-broken, and my mother swooned twice. But even as she was wiping away her tears over the death of my second elder brother, she was also preparing for my wedding. My hope that with his death as a lesson to her she might not suppress me so much was now entirely gone. She would still not allow me to break off my engagement. She had her determination about my marriage, and nothing on earth could induce her to change her mind.

Alas, my dear, dear mother! What a faithful servant you are to the old system. Was it not enough that you had killed my brother, but must you kill me also?

Chapter XXXI

SECRET MEETING

At last a chance came to us. Seeing that we were going to pay homage to the Goddess of Mercy at Chou Yin Nunnery, I was allowed to meet Shiang there. It was the 19th of the 9th moon, supposed to be the third birthday of the year for the Goddess of Mercy. From seven o'clock in the morning a large crowd, mostly women, went to pay their homage with incense and paper money.

As my mother was one of the devoted worshippers of this goddess, she unreservedly allowed me to go out of the house for the day. I suppose she knew that I would probably discuss with Shiang the means of getting away, but I suspect that she had complete confidence in her power to prevent any such scheme being successful when she was keeping watch. She considered that she had me in the hollow of her hand.

Of course the object of my going to this nunnery was not because of my reverence for the goddess, but entirely for a discussion with Shiang about our getting away. In my basket I had some incense sticks, some pieces of sandal-wood and paper-made ingots. On some of the pieces of sandal-wood were pasted pieces of paper on which the words 'Faithful worshipper Hsieh Min Kon makes her reverent bow to the great Goddess of Mercy' were written.

After we had made our hurried offerings to the Goddess, which meant that we had to kneel down four times, we stole away and went to the summit of the mountain. Unfortunately most of the places were crowded with worshippers, who wanted us to write their names on pieces of sandal-wood for them, and it was a long time before we managed to get away after all.

In a peaceful valley surrounded with ancient cedar trees we sat on the ground and had a heart-to-heart talk. The faded yellow leaves falling from the trees were blown by the autumn wind and were dancing everywhere. The sorrowful voice of the cicada, like someone crying all the time, made the atmosphere very miserable.

'Shiang, I never thought that once we were back in our homes we should be enduring a life like this. It is much worse than being in prison!'

I had barely managed to finish this sentence before I was choked with sobs. I could not go on. But Shiang was a girl who seldom shed tears. She heaved a deep sigh, and after a long silence gave me this disappointing reply:

'I, too, never thought that your mother would be so cruel, so obstinate, but since you have come back you will have to be patient. Of course we want to get away, but it will be very difficult!'

'What do you mean by patient? Do you think that you could be patient enough to tolerate what they are going to do to you?'

'Of course not, and I certainly know that you are much less patient than I am, so I am hoping that we can find a very safe and secure way to get away.'

'Yes, I decided to get away a long time ago. I think we shall have to act very quickly. We need not take anything with us. If only we can get out of the tiger's mouth, I am quite willing to become either a beggar or to live on charity, to go from door to door, or to be a slave girl in someone else's family. I would feel that the life would be much happier than my present one. Indeed, I would have no regret even if nobody would engage us to work, or if we could not get enough rice to eat and died of hunger in a strange land. Now let us decide immediately what is the date when we should meet, and the place and the time.'

Before we could finish our conversation my mother sent somebody to look for us. We looked at each other and had to return to our confinement.

As soon as I had made plans for going away I began to change my attitude towards my family. I told my elder sister and sisters-in-law that I had begun to realise that my mother loved me, that my ideas were entirely wrong, that I believed everything had been destined in our previous existence, and that we must not have unreasonable ambitions; that our parents were greater than heaven, and that we should obey their orders absolutely. At first these words sounded incredible to them and my sister asked me:

'You, who have been to school, also believe in a previous existence? I thought you people had no religion.'

'If people who have been to school do not believe in a previous existence and in the gods, how could it happen that the Buddhist classics were written by scholars?'

They smiled and realised that what I said was perfectly true.

Later on my mother began to see that I started to help them to prepare my dresses and so on. She thought I was really surrendering, and once or twice she discussed these things with me.

'As for the dresses, I leave them entirely to you. In whatever style you want them to be cut and made, you just give your orders to the tailors. I only advise that you do not cut your coats too short. They may be very fashionable in the cities, but people in the country are rather old-fashioned and would say that your upper garments were even shorter than your underwear. There are some pieces of satin and silk which I have preserved for you for nearly twenty years. These you should cut for your autumn and winter clothes. I have got these two pieces of red satin which, except for having been made into your coverlets, are still unused. Now when you have children, they would be very useful for making dresses for them.'

At her words I could hardly suppress my laughter. I would very much have liked to tell her: 'Mother, please do not dream in daylight.' But because I wanted to go on with my scheme in secret, I pretended that I was very bashful and looked on the ground.

'Mother, I think it would be better not to cut and make so many dresses, because the mode changes very often and many of them will soon be out of fashion. Neither should you give me so much material. As I will come back to see you from time to time, couldn't I take them gradually when I need them?'

'Here is the place where your caul was buried. Certainly you must come and visit us very often. Nevertheless, to be a bride and not to have many dresses would be looked down upon by others. Many people have to sell their fields and their property to prepare a trousseau for their daughters. When your elder sister's husband's family married off their daughter they had thirty-two silk coverlets and twenty-eight woollen blankets, but I know that they had to sell their rice field to make a show. Although I like to do my best for my daughters, I do not hold that people should really dispose of their property handed down to them by their ancestors in order to be luxurious in the wedding ceremony. If the trousseau is not too modest, that is sufficient.'

'Mother, I remember when you married off my elder sister you were quite extravagant, and I feel that while you, father and mother, have been so economical all your lives, you should really save a little money for your own use later on. Both you and father are getting on, and should enjoy yourselves a little. All I want is to read books, and if my father can give me a few boxes of books at the time of my wedding, I shall be more than satisfied.'

'Good! As the old proverb says: "A good son will not depend upon his father for rice fields and a good daughter will not ask her parents for a trousseau." My child, you are a really worthy descendant of a family which has been thoroughly educated.' My mother said this with a happy smile, and I knew that these words sprang from the bottom of her heart.

My father, too, was very happy when he heard that all I wanted was some of his books. Indeed, he was so happy that his moustache and beard turned up at the ends.

'Good, good! If you really like to study I will give you four big cases of books on philosophy.'

Sometimes in the quietness of midnight I would imagine the disappointment which I was going to cause them, and I would again shed tears on their account.

My father loved my second elder brother and me best. Now that my second elder brother was dead his affection was entirely centred on me. And how about myself? Was I not going to be heart-breaking to him even more than my second elder brother? My mother taught me a song:

'The swallows build their nests by bringing mud from distant places,
 But as soon as the young ones are grown up they disperse and the family is ruined.'

I felt that my father and mother were doing very much the same thing as the swallows, and were taking up mud to build their nest. However, I could not do anything to help them. A person belongs to society, he is no longer simply a devoted son to his parents. Time marches on, and society keeps on advancing. The relation between father and son must not be allowed to hamper the welfare of humanity.

Chapter XXXII

MY FIRST ATTEMPT AT ESCAPE

THIS I can remember very clearly. It was on the 18th of the 10th moon when my aunt Yi Wu invited my parents and me to have an early meal with them. For the last few months, whenever I had been invited out, my mother had at once refused the invitation for me. Now that she had begun to see signs of surrender she had decided to accept the invitation this time, and because on that very day we were having some guests ourselves and she would be very busy the whole morning in preparation for the feast, she herself was not going, but she asked my third elder sister-in-law to accompany me. She termed it very nicely as 'accompanying me,' but in reality it was to keep me under her observation. Of course my father was going too, but a woman would always be more convenient to follow me wherever I went.

'Ha! so you, too, have come!' When I saw that Shiang was also sitting at the table I was so happy that tears almost dropped from my eyes. She, too, was very happy to see me and made me sit next to her.

The feast was given in honour of a bride, and we were guests of lesser importance. Three tables were laid, and two of them were for women and girls. At my table, except for my third elder sister-in-law and the bride, all of us were maidens. We, like our naughty selves, continued to make sport of the bride, and a lady from the next table said to her:

'Bride, do not be afraid of them. These two girls are going to be brides very soon, and you should be very frank in telling them what a future bride should know.'

Her remark made us laugh, and Shiang was blushing.

The feast was excellent. In ordinary cases six dishes are all we would usually have on such an occasion, but to-day there were eight, and they were all well cooked. Everybody was enjoying it heartily and was talking and laughing.

I pinched Shiang's leg, which meant 'March!' Nobody thought that in the twinkling of an eye something would be happening which would make the whole of the village of Hsieh-To-San talk for days.

Wine, cup after cup was filled, and viands, dish after dish came on.

'Ah, I have a stomach-ache!' I put my hands on my stomach and pretended that I was very much troubled.

'I hope you have not eaten something which has disagreed with you. How is it that you have this sudden attack of stomach-ache?'

Many people at the same table put down their chopsticks and stared at me.

'Never mind, I had a little cold last night, and I suppose I have eaten a little too much. I do not think this stomach-ache is very serious. If you will excuse me I will rejoin you later on.'

Saying that I was going to the lavatory, I withdrew, and Shiang, pretending to look after me, followed me out. We came to the lavatory, where I said:

'Let us go. This is the time.'

Chin Chin was the only one who knew that I was going, and she swore that she would not tell anybody. Besides, she had given me a silver dollar, which was her pocket money. It was very kind of her. As we were going Chin Chin rushed up to us with tears in her eyes:

'My elder sister, my uncle, when are you coming back again?' She held our hands and was very reluctant to let us go. Although we were equally reluctant to leave her, we felt as if whips were cracking behind our backs and we dare not stay a moment longer.

'Chin Chin, my good child, do not be sorry. We shall be writing home in a few days.' Turning to Shiang, I said: 'No more delay, let us go at once.'

Coming out of the lavatory, we ran for the little hill behind the house. Two fierce dogs followed us, barking at us very loudly. Immediately a middle-aged woman came from a small house, and as she was looking at us steadily we thought it best to slacken our pace and pretend that we were taking a walk. In order that she should not see through us we had to be very patient, although in our heart of hearts we would have liked to push forward as fast as we could. We felt as though a fire was burning inside us, and we were afraid in case our hostess would discover our long absence, and Shiang's mother would know of our escape by seeing Chin Chin shedding tears. And if anybody reported anything to my mother, she would surely send somebody to chase after us.

'Shiang, let us run. That woman has gone back into her house again.'

Afraid of being overtaken by anybody, we ran with all our might, not daring to look back once. We met one or two coal-miners who knew us, but we pretended that we did not see them and continued our running. We were full of terror, and fearing that we might meet with friends we selected a narrow path between the rice fields, and ran like a couple of criminals such as you might see in the moving pictures. Drops of perspiration rolled down our cheeks and we were out of breath all the time. We felt as if we were two camels with burdens of more than a thousand *catties* on our backs, and we were very fatigued, but we dare not rest for a single second nor slacken our pace in the least.

'Uncle Min, what should we do if somebody were to overtake us?'

Shiang, who was more timid and discreet than I, suddenly stopped running to ask me this.

'Let us run as quickly as possible and they will never overtake us.'

'Never overtake us? They would certainly send some men to chase us, and they would be capable of running much faster than we can.'

'Everybody was very happy at the feast and they would never dream of our running away. If we could only get into a boat sailing from Nan-Tien we would be safe.'

Hill after hill, field after field went past us on either side but we never stopped.

'How happy I am! We have now left the dark place. Good-bye, for ever, my horrible homeland, which is a sample of the old system!' I said this to myself, and soon we arrived at Fu Yin village. From here it is only five *li* to Nan-Tien, and when I looked back and saw nobody was coming after us, I felt like a person who has just escaped the scaffold.

'Shiang, now we are really free!' I said loudly, and jumped with joy.

'Don't be too happy. Wait until the boat sails!' She bent down, and cupping her hands together for some water from the river, she drank and drank. I, too, felt very thirsty after our run, and I also bent down and had a very hearty drink.

'We have only one dollar between us. Will that be sufficient for the boatman?' Shiang was always full of apprehension. Before one question has been solved she would always bring up another.

'Although it will not carry us as far as Changsha, it will take us down the river for some scores of *li*, and will put us out of range of our families. Then we can either beg our way or walk into Changsha. There we can work in some factory, and we can certainly earn our own living.'

Suddenly we thought we heard footsteps behind us and we looked back, but it was only a few ducks paddling in the rice fields.

'Let us finish our journey. It is midday and we might meet some people here.'

We started again and, although we had been born in this part of the country and should know every path in the neighbourhood, we had no time to find a by-path where we could avoid any friends or any passers-by who might detect us. Luckily we met with nobody, and soon we reached the place where the boats started from.

My heavens, were we dreaming or were we in reality! When we were telling the boatman about our journey and the passage money we could afford to pay, I suddenly turned around, to find my mother standing behind me. Two sedan chair bearers were not far away, and they were wiping the sweat from their brows. They pointed and looked at us with smiles.

'All hope is gone,' I said secretly to myself.

My mother would make a very good diplomat. When she saw us in this public place with many people around us she did not in the least betray the fact that she was dealing with a couple of rebel girls. She was not angry in the least. On the contrary, she was full of smiles, and said to the crowd who had begun to gather around us:

'These two girls wanted to be future women scholars. They wanted to study abroad and would not wait another day. As there has been no rain recently it would be a very difficult voyage for them. Don't you think so, my good boatman?'

'Although the river is shallow because of the lack of rain, still I think I could manage to sail all right.' The boatman was very truthful. He did not know how much there was behind this comedy, and he did not really want to lose this business, small though it was.

'As the river is so shallow, certainly the boat would proceed very slowly,' continued my mother with her smile. 'Rather than spend all their days going slowly on the river, it would be much better for them to stay at home and wait for the rain.'

'Young people are always impatient, but haste never really results in speed. I suppose you, madam, want to take them back home.'

'Yes, I want to keep them at home just for a few days more, to enjoy a fine fatted chicken. You see, my good boatman, when they leave their home they will not be able to have such good food as they usually have at home. Excuse me spoiling your business this time, but as soon as the rain comes down I am sure they will come back again.'

The boatman tried to smile, but it was a smile of bitter disappointment.

All the onlookers looked at us and we, like fools, could not find any words to save ourselves. The moment I saw my mother I felt as if my wrists were hand-cuffed and my feet fettered, or, worse still, as if my head was already placed under the guillotine.

Acknowledging my complete defeat, I went home downcast. All that night my mother scolded me, from midnight until morning, and she used all the terrible words she could think of. On the other hand I, like someone dumb, did not say a single word. The next morning my third elder sister-in-law told me what had happened on that day.

'We waited for you to turn up with Shiang, and after more than half an hour we discovered you were not in the house. I went to Shiang's mother to see whether you were there, and she said she had not seen your shadow. Still hoping you might have returned to our home, I went back without finishing the feast. Our mother immediately knew what had happened and said: "I know they have escaped. Get two sedan chair bearers for me immediately and I will find them." She blamed me for being useless, and said that probably I was one of your accomplices, that after all I was not an idol of clay. How could it be possible not to have noticed your absence after such a long interval? She went in the chair immediately after the bearers arrived, and paid no attention whatever to the feast which she was giving later on.'

When I heard the anxiety my mother had and the awful plight she must have been in, I could scarcely suppress my laughter. Although I had not been successful in my first attempt, I had caused her to worry, and I enjoyed thinking of that.

The news that I had run away with Shiang was spread all over the village of Hsieh-To-San, even as far as Nan-Tien, people began to talk about our little episode of escape directly after their usual greetings.

'Those two girls really had courage and cheek. They dared to slip away in the daytime and from a feast where three tables were crowded with people.'

'To think that girls would dare to escape! There is no law and no heaven.'

'Alas, alas! The world is going to the dogs. Everything is changed completely. To think that young maidens would dare to do this kind of disgraceful thing. What is there to be said!'

These were the things people said, and they were all carefully conveyed to my ear, but I did not care. I did not regard them as insults. A Revolutionary should be prepared to suffer anything— that was the thought which comforted me.

After I came back from my attempted escape my life was even less free than before. Chin Chin was not allowed to see me again, and even my sister and sisters-in-law and my aunt were not allowed to visit me.

At night I would watch through my little window a small space of sky as blue as a sapphire with a moon as pure as jade. From the distance I could hear the barking of the dogs. I felt that I would end my days here.

This life was more unbearable than being shut up in a proper prison, where one could meet many fellow sufferers to whom one might breathe one's hardships. One might talk of the past and of dreams for the future, but now, in solitary confinement alone in a tiny room, the only thing one could do was to shut one's mouth and reflect in silence. But I was not going to be a gentle lamb to be slaughtered at any time my master desired. I had tried once, I would try a second time and third time, indeed, endless times.

Chapter XXXIII

SECOND ATTEMPT

On a dark night drizzling with rain I made my second attempt to escape. On the preceding day my mother had been packing my cases and was very tired, so she went to bed much earlier than usual. When I could hear her loud snores very distinctly, I suddenly thought of escape again.

There were two doors to my room. The one on the right was now locked, and the one on the left led to my mother's room, and this was bolted every night from her side. I could not climb out of the windows because they had been recently barred with heavy planks. However, I knocked on the door of my mother's room and said I was very thirsty and wanted a drink. Luckily it was my father who got up to open the door, and he never thought that I was trying to make my escape. I told him I was going to have a drink in my third elder sister-in-law's room, because she always kept hot water in her room for the requirements of her baby in the night. My father saw that I went into her room and thought all was well.

I told my sister-in-law that I had permission to spend the night with her because I was very frightened after having a terrible dream. At last my third elder sister-in-law consented to let me sleep in her bed and she thought that I would be quite safe with her. She must have been awake during the early part of the night, for when she fell asleep again she was soon snoring very loudly. The rain became very heavy and the whole world was wrapped in complete darkness. I realised that the loving mother who had been troubled by her child for the best part of the night was not likely to be easily awakened, so I crept up very silently and ran out as quickly as I could. This time I tried not to go by the road to Nan-Tien, so the only way was for me to tramp over the mountain.

When I was groping for the dark mountain, a dog started to bark at me. I immediately realised that I must walk like a gentleman and not like a thief, so I slackened my pace and made my way to the mountain. As if the heavens were taking pity on me, the rain began to stop and there was a shade of paleness in the sky which enabled me to see my road very clearly. The dogs were still barking but not so fiercely as before. I walked boldly forward, and as the mountain path was very rocky and steep it was very difficult to walk, especially in the rain, as it was slippery. I fell many times, and was covered with clay and water. I thought that with mud all over my face I would be taken as a ghost if I met anybody in the morning.

As soon as I got out of the village I began to run again, and I felt as if there were thousands of people chasing behind me.

Suddenly I fell into the brook, and as I fell I felt my face was covered with blood, being cut in several places by the gravel. 'Oh heavens, please save me ! My life and death depend upon you. If I do not get away to-night my life will be finished.'

I do not believe in heaven, but when one is in a desperate state one's thought naturally turns towards something which is supposed to be powerful.

In the distance I seemed to see some stars sparkling. At first I thought they were real stars, but soon realised that on a dark night like this one couldn't see any stars. Then the red stars became bigger and nearer, and I started wondering what they were. Were they fireflies or were they ghost fires? I was told that in the wild places where people were buried one generally saw ghost fires.

Thoughts of terror began to come into my mind. Would they be devils trying to frighten me back to my home? No, it must be my imagination. I should not be afraid. I must go on, and I should realise that at this time of night, and on such a night, there was nothing to stop me from proceeding on my journey.

But the sparkling lights came nearer and nearer to me, and I kept on wondering whether they were caused by human beings or by ghosts. As they were coming directly in my way, had I better avoid them or have the matter out by going straight into them? I thought for a moment that if it was a ghost, it might be the ghost of my second elder brother who came to guide me. I thought that he would never forsake me, especially at such a time when I needed him most. But really I never believed in the theory of the survival of the soul, and stories of ghosts were mere nonsense.

Then suddenly I began to see that two big torches were beaming in front of me, and someone shouted very loudly:

'Hey, look! There she is, there she is!'

I turned immediately and started to run in the opposite direction. No matter whether they were ghosts or men, I wanted to get away from them.

'Young Mistress Min, don't run away. We have come to fetch you back. Your mother was worrying in case you would be frightened on such a night.'

My heavens! I was right after all. They were two devils who had been sent to bring me back to hell again. Couldn't they realise that they were really acting as instruments for the ruler of the other world?

No matter what I said to them they were very calm, and tried their best to persuade me to go home. I was furious, and used very strong language to them. They had at last to drag me home by force.

When I was quite near my prison, I began to see that the big black dog was their guide, and that it was owing to this dog that I was found.

Everybody at home was up, and even the lamp before the ancestral shrine was lighted, as if they were celebrating the New Year's Eve.

'Where did you find this devil? Do not bring her in, but throw her out. I do not want to look at her!' my mother shouted, and she herself looked more hideous than death. My poor third elder sister-in-law, trembling and with swollen eyes, greeted me. I looked at her with sympathy and gratitude. Undoubtedly she had helped me in my escape; although I had failed again miserably it was entirely because of her that I was able to make this second attempt.

CHAPTER XXXIV

THIRD ATTEMPT

TWENTY days more and I would be married. The Shiao family had sent many telegrams to their son to come home for the great event but he did not appear, because I, too, had sent a message to him on my first arrival at Nan-Tien, telling him that I would not marry him. The parents of both families were greatly worried, and they were comparable to ants on a hot oven, uncomfortable in the daytime as well as at night. My mother was particularly so; she could not eat, could not drink, suffering sleepless nights, cursing me and grumbling to my father saying he should not have sent me to school.

Their worst fear was in case Shiao Kwang would not take me as his wife. That indeed would have been a greater shame than my not consenting to marry him. While my mother was preparing everything for the bride, I told my father very frankly:

'If you think you may be able to take me to the Shiao family by force, there will be only one of two results, either I will commit suicide or I will escape. Father, I sincerely advise you to believe that since I will carry out my words, you had better not send all those things to them. It will be just pure waste.'

My father believed me, and conveyed what I said to my mother. With the experience of my repeated attempts to escape, he believed that I could not possibly marry Shiao Kwang. But my mother had her obstinate views.

'To commit suicide! That was a mere threat. Every young girl is liable to threaten her parents if she doesn't get a husband to her taste. To escape! When she is married she will think better of that. When a woman is in a man's hands, no matter how fierce she was before, she will become as gentle as a lamb. I believe our future son-in-law is not a fool. If he would only be nice to her, I am sure she would take to him in spite of her threats.'

Alas, my mother was too clever to understand her daughter's feelings and character. She thought that with this splendid trousseau and some nice promises she might induce me to do her bidding, so ten days before the wedding she sent everything to the Shiao family. I sighed. I was deeply sorry for her. I was the only one who realised that she had been saving for more than ten years, and now all her savings were given away to somebody who would not be married to her daughter.

For the third time I attempted to escape. But as my sister said very wisely, no matter how capable I was, I could not possibly fly out of my mother's cage.

This time my mother did not send two strong farm hands to chase me, but two gentlemen in their long garments. One was my eldest brother and the other my sister's husband. When they stopped me outside a shop in a street in Nan-Tien I took out a sharp knife which I carried with me and put it near my throat. I swore to them very solemnly:

'I have sworn that if anybody comes to force me home, I will cut my throat there and then.'

But in the twinkling of an eye my knife passed into the hands of my eldest brother. He also put it near his throat and said:

'I will kill myself if you do not come with me.'

'And me too,' added my sister's husband.

Immediately a great crowd gathered around us because, in order to get away unobserved, I had disguised myself as a middle-aged woman, and I suppose my disguise was so ridiculous that people were staring at me with curiosity. When I was arguing with my brother and my sister's husband the whole street was blocked up by onlookers, and they began to laugh at me when they saw that I was shedding tears and struggling desperately with my men folk. For two hours we kept on arguing and struggling, and at last I was persuaded to go home for the time being. As I knew I could not go any further, and I did not want to make myself a laughing-stock to the whole town, I had to follow them.

Strangely enough, this time when I arrived home my mother did not say a word to me. Father, after giving me a very hurried glance, looked down at the ground and went away. The house was again crowded with people and I could hear whispers from every-one that I thought must be comments on my disguise. They wanted to laugh but they dared not provoke me. My niece, Yun Pao, was the only one who said audibly:

'Mamma, why is auntie dressed in such queer clothes?'

My sister shook her head at her and the child dare not say another word.

I was not going to be silent this time. I was only waiting for someone to say a word to me, and then I would go for her with my last breath. But unexpectedly everyone was as if deaf and dumb, and my mother tried her best to avoid me. I went to bed by myself.

The wedding day was approaching, and Shiao Kwang had not yet come home. To the repeated telegrams sent to him his answer was always, 'Telegrams received. Returning later.' The Shiao family was so desperately anxious to have the wedding performed that they decided to take me to their home on that very day even if the bridegroom should not arrive. They said that they could perform the wedding ceremony by proxy, and as soon as their son arrived a second ceremony could take place. At first I thought that my mother would consent to this arrangement, but she knew that I would escape from the Shiao family immediately I was there, and that would be a very great damage to her good name, so she insisted that the wedding must not take place before the boy's arrival. A few days later the go-between came in a sedan chair and bowed repeatedly to my mother:

'Congratulations! Congratulations! The bridegroom has arrived at last!'

Immediately every member of my family was as busy as if they had just been mobilised, but my sister and my third elder sister-in-law came secretly to my room and shed a tear of sympathy. They sighed and were very sorry for me. They were afraid that something tragic would happen on the eve of the wedding.

'Alas! You must think very carefully before you do anything rash. You must remember that you are a well-educated girl, and you must not sacrifice your knowledge even if you have no love for your own life.'

My third elder sister-in-law said this to me. My sister was sobbing incessantly. She could not find words to comfort me. My eldest sister-in-law and my sixth great-aunt came to persuade me not to be obstinate, and to congratulate me on the coming great event. When they said, 'The Goddess of Mercy will protect you,' I felt that remark to be almost unendurable and would have liked to answer:

'Let the Goddess of Mercy protect you! I have no need of her because I shall become a goddess myself very soon.'

The children were jumping and running about and laughing

in the big hall, where red lanterns with red candles inside them were hanging everywhere. The Shiao family had been very generous in sending plenty of candles to us, and the children were enjoying these things very much.

Everybody in Hsieh-To-San was more or less full of apprehension. They did not know whether this would turn out to be a tragedy or a comedy. All they knew was that a monster—a rebel female—was going to do something extraordinary that would furnish them with material for gossip after their tea and wines. I was the talk of the whole village. They wanted to criticise me, discuss me, and even speculate what would be my future. Shiang's mother had also been invited by my mother to come and partake of the wedding feast. As she knew that I had been attempting to escape three times before, she said this to me:

'Min Kon, you have been troubling yourself unnecessarily for the past month. Look into the mirror and you will realise that a bride should take care of herself much better than you have done. I advise you to give up your wild thoughts.'

Shiang, at her side, also said:

'Uncle Min, I think you had better give it up. There is no hope of escape.'

I was furious, and when I was alone with her I said:

'So you have become a coward.'

'I have no more strength for struggle. I have decided to let myself be destroyed by the old system.'

'Why have you suddenly become a coward.'

'Because my strength has failed me.'

'All right! You will become a model woman, and will act entirely according to your father's and mother's instructions, and believe in the plausible words of the go-betweens. You will become an excellent wife.'

I thought that these words would provoke her, but the only result they produced was that she laughed at me ironically and asked me sarcastically:

'Please tell me, what is the result of your struggle?'

'The result? You will see!'

I was very sorry to perceive that we two, who had grown up together and become friends later on, were now no better than enemies. The friendship between us was entirely gone. While I looked down on her, perhaps she was also looking down on me.

Both of us believed that the other was not acting properly. We looked at each other in silence for a few seconds, then both turned our eyes away and looked at the fire.

That was our last meeting. When I made my fourth attempt at escape and succeeded at last in leaving my old village, I knew I was fighting by myself. Since then Shiang has become a martyr to the old system and the mother of three children. I think of her very often and pity her all the more.

When I succeeded in getting away for the last time I was not in a hurry, and like the poet who lingered in the beautiful scene of his childhood, I composed this poem:

> 'Farewell, my native land;
> A place of beauty, with mountains evergreen,
> With water always murmuring;
> With peach and apricot trees like pictures,
> And with weeping willows hanging down like threads.
>
> 'O, my beautiful native land,
> You have intoxicated the soul of my childhood,
> And have also wasted away the best time of my life.
> There is nothing left but bloody scars on my heart.
>
> 'The old system was like a fierce tiger
> Who would swallow everyone in the darkness.
> Struggle! struggle!
> That alone will bring the final victory everywhere.
> Farewell, my native land!'

Part Five

MY WANDERING LIFE

Chapter XXXV

IN PRISON

PERHAPS I was destined to taste all sorts of bitterness in this world. Just coming out from the family prison, I was going to another prison very soon, and this time it was a real one.

When I was in Changsha I thought of poor Shiang, who was caged in a tiny place and could have little fresh air, so I bought some books about Socialism which I thought might be helpful to her to pass her long and dreary days. I had them packed and was going to the post office, when suddenly I met two young men.

'Min, where are you going?' said one. 'I never thought to meet you here. When did you arrive?'

One was O Se and the other was Mo Lin, two comrades in the days of Wu Chang. We stopped amid the traffic and talked about what had happened since we parted. They told me they were staying at Shin An Hotel, and so we decided to have a talk there.

Everything happened as if in a dream. While we were talking about old times, soldiers and policemen rushed in, took my parcel of books together with some of their books, bound us, and escorted us to their headquarters. They gave us no reason and no chance of explaining ourselves. On the way all the people in the street stopped to look at us, and some children even shouted at us:

'Kill them, kill them, those Communists!'

And I heard an elderly lady say with a sigh :

'What a pity that one of those wretched Communists is a young girl.'

'Walk quickly. Are your legs not functioning?' One of the soldiers struck me with the butt of his rifle very hard.

'You devil! How dare you strike me?' I stopped and looked at him fiercely.

'M'm, strike you! I shall cut off your head to-morrow!'

I was urged to push forward, and I don't know how I possibly got into the headquarters.

We were locked into the prison immediately. It was composed of two small rooms. The two men occupied one, and I was put in the smaller and darker room with a stinking smell.

'Hey, what is that?'

I thought I was treading on something soft, and someone immediately shouted:

'It is a person like yourself,' and she stood up.

'I am extremely sorry. Coming just from outside and the room being so dark I cannot see at all. I hope you will pardon me.' My sincerity moved her.

'Never mind. I was having a nap just then. What is your case?' Her voice indicated that she was not from Changsha, probably coming from Lui Yang.

'I have no case. They just arrested me without reason.'

'From where did they arrest you?'

'From a hotel. I went to see two friends, and the inspector suddenly came with soldiers and police and without asking me any questions, they arrested me.'

'Where are they?'

'Also here in the room opposite.' Following the pointing of my finger she looked and saw Mo Lin and O Se.

'Which of them is your husband?'

I thought this was ridiculous, and would have liked to rebuff her, but realising that we were both fellow sufferers I was not angry.

'They are both my friends. I am still a maiden.'

This was the first moon of the year. It was drizzling with rain and everywhere was wet. We sat on a board, not covered with a mattress, but merely with some rotten straw. Neither were we given coverlets nor blankets. No food was served to us. I felt a thousand things were stinging me, and I preferred to stand rather than to sit or lie down.

'The straw has been here for a very long time. I think there must be plenty of fleas and bugs in it. I am full of bites.'

She tried to show me her arm by pulling up her sleeve, but it was so dark that I could see nothing.

'Are we having nothing to eat at all?' I felt hungry and I was hoping that she would say 'Yes.'

'M'm, something to eat? You are not given even a drop of water to drink. You must inform your family, and ask them to send you rice and tea.'

'Oh, so it is like that? But my family will not be sending me anything.'

The jailer came and swore at us and told us to shut up.

About seven o'clock in the evening several soldiers with pistols in their hands came. They opened the lock and took me to the judge.

The judge was a man little more than forty years old, with a moustache in the form of an inverted V. He looked like a very kind man, but reason told me that judges are never kind.

He asked me my surname, my age, my profession and my native place, and then his next sentence was:

'How were you initiated into the Communist Party? Where is your organisation, and what specific work are you in charge of?'

'What? I do not understand what you mean. I am only a student from the Girls' Normal School.'

He said that it was no use for me to give a cunning answer to his question, and he added:

'If you are not a Communist, why is it that you have these Communistic books?'

'I bought these books from a shop. If it is wrong to have them, then you must arrest the booksellers, because they must be Communists too.'

'Don't talk nonsense. Confess immediately, and I promise you that you will be released. Otherwise you will be shot to-morrow morning.' The judge threatened me with angry looks, and wanted me to confess.

'My life is entirely in your hands. If you want to shoot me, I cannot do anything about it, but I have nothing to confess,' I answered very calmly, but he was still angry.

'We will not shoot anybody who is innocent. Because you have offended against the law, you are liable to be shot.'

'I have not committed any offence against the law.'

'The proofs are here.' He banged the books on the table. 'How dare you deny it? Strike her, strike her!' he shouted to the man standing at my side.

Thick and heavy blows were inflicted on my legs. I fell down. Although it was very painful, I maintained silence.

'If you still do not confess, then we will pour chili water into your nostrils.'

I had already heard that this was one of the cruel tortures they used against Communists, and many political prisoners who really were not Communists were made to confess simply because of not being able to endure this hardship. Many young lives had been wrongfully sacrificed.

They immediately saw that I was thinking hard. Indeed, I was trembling.

'Confess immediately! Do not try to think of something to deceive me. Do you want a dose of chili water?'

'You cannot frighten me into a false confession. I know nothing and have nothing to confess.'

I do not know what the clerk wrote in the book. The judge looked at it and said:

'Wait for another time. We will let her taste something bitter.' And I was ordered to be sent back to my confinement.

When I was near the door of their prison, Mo Lin put his head near the iron bars and said:

'What did you say?'

When I was on the point of answering him, a pistol butt knocked very heavily on my shoulder and I was told to shut up. They, too, had been summoned before the judge separately. It seemed that the case was very serious, because I heard one of the jailers say to the night watchman:

'The judge said one of them is an important member of the Communist Party, and he will be shot to-morrow morning.'

The woman was sound asleep. When I stood up behind the bars to look at my friends, they too looked at me in despair. We could only communicate our thoughts with our eyes, we were not allowed to use our mouths. I noticed that in O Se's eyes tears glistened in the dim light. I began to think that he should not be like this. In our school were we not taught: 'A revolutionary will not shed tears, but only blood'? Why was it that when something unfortunate happened the first thing he shed should be tears?

Chapter XXXVI

OUT OF PRISON

I WAS summoned before the judge for a second time, and what I said to him was exactly like I had said before.

I perceived that the judge was very angry with me but he suppressed his anger, and instead of beating me again or giving me other forms of torture, he asked me very politely to come to his private office. There he dismissed his attendant and talked to me alone. I knew he was trying the way of soft tactics. He wanted to use some sweet honeyed words, as he would to a child, in order to induce me to confess.

'Sit down, please, and let us discuss this slowly. Do you smoke?'

'No, thank you.'

'Nowadays many young people are going in the wrong direction, and therefore sacrificing their lives in vain. I see that you are a very clever and extraordinary girl, and it must have been in a moment of weakness of mind that you drifted on to the wrong road. If you will realise your mistake and determine to reform, I have very good hopes for you in the future. I am really one of your well-wishers, and will do everything to help you. Now, please tell me very honestly about yourself.'

Although his words were so kind, there seemed to be two deadly rays shining from his fierce eyes. I dare not look at him, and turning away I said:

'I am sorry, judge, I do not quite understand what you are saying. I have not been drifting on to the wrong road, and so I have nothing to reform.'

'Do you want to be beheaded?' He banged one of his fists on the table, which made me jump. He was very angry and did not pretend he was not.

'If you want to behead me, I cannot help it. Many things cannot be helped, however much one wishes they could.'

I also became angry, and said this loudly. As he could not find out anything more from me, he ordered that I should be fettered, and I was conducted back to my cell again.

On the following morning, when my fellow sufferer awoke, she put her mouth near to my ear and whispered:

'How many times were you summoned last night?'

I whispered back to her, revealing what had occurred. She shook her head and heaved a deep sigh.

'Before, I was here for seven days, and I saw five young girls like you, and one of them was only fifteen. They were all put in prison on the first day and led away the following morning to be . . . Alas! I hope you will not . . . be like that!'

I did not know how to answer.

Then she told me about herself. She said her case was not a serious one, only that she had wounded her husband in a quarrel. She added:

'As soon as I get out I will send you rice and tea. Please do not despair. I think I shall be out in a few days.'

'I am afraid I shall not need anything from you by that time!' I said this rather absent-mindedly, and I never thought it would make her shed tears for me. I was deeply moved. I held her hand very fast and put my head on her breast. In the meantime my tears were running down in streams. I felt she was a very endearing person, and I treated her as a very old friend.

I never dreamt that I, who could be considered as having my name down in the Book of the King of the Other World, would at last be allowed to come back again.

When I was summoned for the fourth time the judge told me that all our statements were considered to be stubborn. He told me that they had found further evidence of a Communist nature in O Se's suitcase, and that as we were all people of no profession and coming from places which we couldn't vouch for, we should be sentenced to death.

Then the judge started to ask me to state the conditions of my family in detail, and when he heard the name of my father he was shocked. He told me that he had been a student under my father for four years, and because of this relationship between him and my father there was a ray of hope for saving my life.

He immediately promised to let me write a letter to my eldest brother, who was now living outside the North City Gate, and very kindly ordered the serving soldier to despatch the letter. About three o'clock on the following day my eldest brother and his father-in-law, Mr. Kung, came hurriedly to see me in prison.

Of course my eldest brother pulled a long face and gave me a very good lecture, but elderly Mr. Kung was very kind and comforted me thus:

'Do not worry. No matter what happens we will get you out of this.'

'I am not alone. I have two friends who are here.' Mo Lin and O Se smiled and nodded their heads to them. But my eldest brother said sarcastically:

'Since they have come here they must be patient and taste a little bit of life behind iron bars. Few people are so privileged.'

They went to see the judge, and I said to my friends:

'There is some hope we might get out.'

'Since the judge was a student under your father, of course there is hope for you, but for us I do not know.' O Se said this in a very sad voice and his eyes were full of tears.

'If we must die, let us die. What do I care!' Mo Lin started up sentimentally, but I tried to comfort him.

'If I am released, of course you will be released. Our case is the same.'

After two hours my eldest brother came back alone. He told me that as soon as security from a responsible shop could be obtained I would be set free.

'How about my two friends?' I asked anxiously.

'That I don't know. As I do not know them personally, naturally I dare not say anything for them. It is entirely beyond my power to do anything for them.' He said this very loudly in order that they might hear him.

'No, I will not go out alone. I will stay in prison and keep them company,' I said resolutely.

'To keep them company? If their lives . . .'

'Then I will also sacrifice my life with them.'

'Why?'

'Because it was on account of a few books I bought that we were arrested. Actually I have compromised them. Why should I be released while they are still in jail?'

I knew I was right, and I also knew that my eldest brother, because of me, would not really let them alone. Since the judge was a student under my father, there should be some consideration for all of us.

But very fortunately O Se's friend, Len Chun, had heard the

news of our arrest and had come with a shop security to get them out. So on the fourth day all three of us had our freedom.

We had spent three days in prison, and all we had eaten was a bowl of noodles each, and that cost us two dollars. It was wretched stuff, but it tasted better than the finest dish in any splendid banquet at which I have ever been. Even to this day I can remember its nice taste in my mouth.

After we got out of prison we never saw each other again. I was told later that their departure was miserable. The only person who saw them off was Len Chun, who told me that they were still worrying about me in case I would be made to go back to my home. I was very grateful to them for their friendship even in the time of their own distress.

Chapter XXXVII

THE SCHOOLMISTRESS

'Good news! Mr. Chang, the headmaster of the Fifth Provincial Middle School, would like you for a teacher for the Chinese class in the elementary school attached to the middle school. I have recommended you to him, and as he knew us very well, he engaged you immediately. Now, pack up your things and start for Heng Yang to-morrow.'

My eldest brother told me this happy news, and I was over-joyed. My heavens, I hoped this was not a dream!

This was the spring of 1928. My original idea was first of all to find some work, and if the opportunity arose I would like to go to work in a school. As for entering a university for higher studies, that was only a dream which I knew would never be realised, but nevertheless there was such a hope in my mind, and I would never give it up. Of course, in the first place I wanted to be independent and not be an expense either to my family or to my friends, and secondly, there was no other way open to me, so I immediately resigned myself to the life of a miserable school-teacher.

When I arrived at the school, the headmaster put me in touch with Mr. Huan the teacher in charge of the elementary school. Immediately I perceived that I didn't make a very good first impression on him. He never thought that Mr. Chang would engage such a young girl to teach such an important class, Chinese being the mother-tongue of the children. As a rule people always thought that young girls were useless. They could make trouble but achieve nothing. And the chief of the elementary school shared this view. To be a teacher at all is a thing which frightens me. The room assigned to me was next to the class which I was going to teach. It was the second term of the sixth year and the second term of the fifth year combined in one class, and I was the form mistress.

'My heavens! To-morrow I shall be a schoolmistress. What am I to do?' On the preceding afternoon I leaned on the balustrade outside my room, looking at the sky, and was in a quandary. I did not have a comfortable night, and was looking with misgiving for the approach of the day. Though I love children, for the time being I forgot about them and could only think of my miseries.

Why was it that I could not be like others, and have a chance of going into a university for further studies, but should have to resign myself to this miserable life of playing with a piece of chalk all day long?

What ability and what qualifications had I to be a teacher of the rising generation? I kept on asking myself.

The dreadful day arrived. I had been told by the headmaster that I was the form mistress, and it was my responsibility to be present at the morning meeting before the classes began, to say something to the students and to look after them, and on the days when I was on special duty I had to call the rolls in the morning and afternoon, inspect the dormitories and classrooms, record the proceedings of the day in the classroom diaries, and I must not leave the office the whole day. Should there arise any quarrels between the students, or if they had any requirements, it was my duty to attend to them.

These details made me very uneasy. I do not think I am good at these things, and there was no way of asking about them.

The morning meeting started.

Like a puppet I stood in the playground. The whistle sounded and all the children were listening intently to what the teacher on duty that day was saying. Suddenly all their small eyes looked at me, which made me very embarrassed. My face was burning, and I turned my head away to look at the basket-ball board. No, that was wrong. The headmaster told me that I should look at the students during the morning meeting, so I had to turn my head back. Ah, that was dreadful! More than three hundred pairs of eyes were staring at me as if they were counting how many hairs I had on my head. I cannot say why I was afraid, but I only wished that I was not there.

Another whistle sounded and the students began to march. This made me much easier and, following the students of the fifth and sixth year, I entered the classroom.

When I stepped on the platform I realised that I must be blushing because I felt very hot.

'My schoolmates, I too am a schoolgirl coming recently from Normal School. Actually I am not a graduate yet, because I joined the Army during my last year at my school, and therefore I have not obtained the diploma. According to my age, I am not qualified to be your teacher, but I think I shall make a very good and sincere friend for you all. If there is anything which you do not understand, I do not presume to be able to teach you, but we can have a general discussion and study the subject together. Therefore I hope you will treat me like one of your schoolmates rather than as a teacher.'

After my short speech the children began to smile on me, and from that moment onwards I became their teacher, and also a slave for my living.

It was not so bad. Though the teaching occupied most of my time when I should have been studying, my mind was very much at ease, and every sentence uttered by the children, every movement made by them, was always lovely to me. They were so innocent, so pure, so honest that I had to like them.

As a new member of society I was a complete failure, for I did not know how to be hypocritical, how to say things which I did not mean, or how to do things which I did not want to do. I was always honest and frank to everybody. Alas, I knew too little of the world, and because of this something unfortunate happened soon after I came to this school.

All the teachers in the school were men and I was the only mistress, and because I was very young and the class I took was the highest of the elementary school, I did not get on very well with my fellow teachers, especially the one who was in charge of this school. As I was almost a child myself, and liked to mix with them all day long in their play, my students liked and respected me more than they did any other teacher. They also were most obedient to me and paid special attention to my classes.

They liked very much to talk with me, and whenever I told them about the Revolution of 1927 they would jump with joy. Some of the boys who were members of the Boy Scouts had been giving lectures to the people outside. They also told me how heartily they were welcomed by their listeners. It seemed to me that these past incidents about the Revolution became more interesting when they were related by the children.

I began to know that Mr. Wong was a young man with advanced ideas. He realised what an age we were in and understood the Revolution thoroughly. We began to talk to each other, as he was also a form master and had a profound knowledge of classical education as well as a grasp of the new knowledge. We had much to talk about together. To be truthful, besides him there was not another person with whom I liked to talk. But I was teaching for twenty-eight hours a week, besides having to correct the children's diaries, handwriting, notebooks and compositions. I also must read a little bit myself and prepare for my lessons. What more time could I spare for talking?

Because I loved the children, I paid special attention to their school life and looked after them in every way. For instance, the library, gymnasium and games room should all have been extended. I tried my best to get the school authorities to buy more books and more equipment for the children. The school library was a miserable place. Besides a few old-fashioned magazines and nonsensical novels, there was nothing at all. They had only two footballs, which had been patched and patched again, and as for the games room, there was nothing except a set of ping-pong, and that had been bought by the students themselves. In connection with my proposals for further equipment, I made repeated requests to the teacher in charge of the elementary school, and these made him very angry with me. One day the headmaster asked me to see him.

'The teacher in charge of the elementary school, Mr. Huan, is not satisfied with you. I do not know what is the matter. Perhaps when young people first come to serve in society they are a little bit too frank and forward, and that is a handicap.' He was quite uneasy, and could not find suitable words to say to me.

'What, I am not satisfactory? It is probably not that I am too frank and forward, but that I have been too honest, too responsible and too enthusiastic about my work. Tell me what I should do.'

Honestly I did not know what to do. I thought that to be enthusiastic about one's work was a thing to be recommended.

'You are putting to me a very difficult question, but I think the best answer would be to advise you to take everything more easily. Wait until the end of the term and see what we can do.'

'Do you want me to resign after the term?'

'M'm, I am afraid so.'

'What is your reason?'

'Well, you have been on rather intimate terms with a certain master. As this is an out-of-the-way city, people are not accustomed to such freedom. Of course this is just one of Mr. Huan's pretexts. His real aim is to get rid of you . . .'

'What is it, please,' I interrupted.

'To be honest, he is afraid of you because you are more capable and more responsible and, above all, more respected by the students.'

'I know. That is a very serious shortcoming on my part, but his pretext is not a very good one. Since this is a co-education school and you have engaged a schoolmistress, how would it be possible for me to avoid being friendly with a schoolmaster? Besides, I have only talked with Mr. Wong two or three times, and our conversation was entirely concerned with literature.'

'I know, but it would be better if you could avoid discussing even that with him. If you could do that, he would have no pretext!'

'Ha, ha! that is quite easy,' and I laughed.

From the next day I put into practice my own Monroe doctrine. Not only did I not speak with any of the schoolmasters, but neither would I enter the masters' common-room, nor partake in the masters' committee meetings. My excuse was that as all the others were men and I should not speak with any man, I had better avoid them altogether. When I started with this policy, of course I knew that they would begin to talk about me, and Mr. Wong felt that I had not been fairly treated. There were many other masters who had sympathy for me, but still I decided not to communicate with them at all.

One evening the teacher in charge of the elementary school paid me an unexpected visit. I would have liked to turn him out, but he had already sat down in my room.

'What is your business here, Mr. Huan?'

'No particular business. Just to have a talk with you.'

'I am sorry, but I do not want to talk with any master.'

'Ah, ha! you want me to go? Well, I will go.' He looked at me with a fierce smile.

'I hope you will.'

'But I am thinking, since you have such driving energy and such good teaching methods, that you should not waste your time here with us.'

I knew what he was going to say, but I pretended that I did not understand.

7 *

'Waste my time? Indeed! I am doing some good work here, and besides, I am being paid for it.'

'Well said, well said! But for a scholar with a future like you the best way is to acquire further education. This school is a wretched place for you to waste your time in.'

'All right, I understand. I would not have cared to come to your school had I not been asked by my friend, Mr. Chang, the headmaster. Since you have such good wishes for my welfare and my future, I can assure you that I will leave the school when the summer vacation comes. Good-bye, I do not want to see you again.'

Later on I learned that he had a relative who was out of a job, and was hoping that I would leave the school sooner. I was sorry that my staying in the place was depriving somebody of an honest bowl of rice, so I decided to leave the school as soon as possible.

Ten days before the ceremony of graduation of the sixth form, which I had been teaching, I left the school silently, but my students knew that I was going and they came to bid me farewell, and many of them shed tears.

'We will meet in future. I hope you will be diligent in your studies.' My eyes also became red, and I had nothing to say. I gave them a last long look and went away.

I had twenty dollars with me, and the school still owed me one month's salary, but I wanted to get away hurriedly, and could not wait for another month for overdue money.

CHAPTER XXXVIII

UNDER SUSPICION

MY first experience of the ways of the world was a severe blow to me. I began to see that it was a dark place, and many of its principles were horrible. Hypocrisy was everywhere. How terrible it was!

I had also seen that the old system was still prevailing in all parts of China, and that women, and especially unmarried girls, had a slender chance in the world. But I was not in despair. I took this as one of my first lessons, and a very good lesson too, and I was ready to take more, so that I would really be able to face the horrible reality of life. I must not give up my struggle and surrender to the old system. Let me go forward. The world is large. I could always find, away from Changsha, a place where I could fight and maintain my ground.

I decided not to let anybody know of my whereabouts, and to start my wandering life. Like a fallen leaf in the autumn wind, I would stay wherever I drifted to.

There was a girl who was in similar circumstances to mine. She was I Chin. She had written me many letters asking me to take her out of Changsha. She had been nearly murdered by the old system, and if I did not help her nobody would do so. So I sent her a letter asking her to go with me to Shanghai, to work in some factory if we could not find anything better to do.

Len Chun, who was in Changsha, gave me all his sympathy. He told me the boat I should take, and where I could find friends. As I had left the school in a very unsatisfactory manner, I decided that I must leave Changsha without letting my eldest brother know. He would blame me for not being sociable with the authorities of the school to which he had recommended me, and would not understand that I wanted to start on my adventurous wandering life.

In the evening I, with I Chin and Len Chun, embarked on a boat bound for Wu Chang. I Chin was exactly like an escaped convict, fearing lest somebody from her family was following her. Len Chun, too, said that this trip was a rather risky one, for the military law prevailing in Changsha paid strict attention to all travellers who were suspected as Communists. He tried to divert our thoughts by telling us amusing stories, but we were still full of terror.

'Hark! Is that the police coming to inspect us?' I heard a noise outside and asked Len Chun and I Chin to stop talking. I looked through the crevice of the cabin door and saw a group of policemen and soldiers on board starting their search. Len Chun was also frightened, and he said, knitting his brows:

'Don't be frightened. Let us have an alibi.'

He was a man of the world. Although he realised that the search would be troublesome, he assumed a very calm attitude.

'What is an alibi?' I Chin asked me in a whisper.

'An alibi is a story we should tell to the police.' Len Chun lighted a cigarette and we sat down to make up a story. He was very quick, and within ten minutes he had told us what we were to say and to stick to.

I remembered what had happened to me here in this city a few months ago. I was afraid that I would compromise I Chin and Len Chun, and asked them to go back and leave me alone to face my misfortunes.

'Mr. Len Chun, you had better go home now, and you too, I Chin. It is better for you not to be with me, in case the police and the soldiers should start trouble with me again. I do not want to compromise you.'

Before Len Chun could say anthing, I Chin burst into tears.

'If you don't want me to go with you, I will jump into the Shiang River and commit suicide. How could you, my sister Min! Haven't I told you there is no other way for me but death? Wherever you go I will follow you.'

I Chin's tears were dropping on my heart. I could not say anything. What were we to do?

'Do not cry. If anybody hears you crying they will knock at the door to find out what is the matter.' Len Chun tried to stop I Chin crying by frightening her.

'Of course,' I continued, 'I wanted to save you, so I told you we should get away from here, but I am worrying in case anything befalls me again like it did a few months ago. How could I forgive myself for dragging you into something which was no concern of yours?'

While I Chin was still sobbing, Len Chun assumed an attitude of an elder brother trying to comfort his little sister. He said:

'Do not be too complicated with your thoughts. Calm yourself. I do not think there is anything serious. In all probability you will have a very peaceful night, and to-morrow morning when the sirens sound you will be on your way to freedom, leaving the sea of suffering behind you.'

'Bang! Bang! Bang! Loud knocks were suddenly heard on the door.

'Who is there?' I asked, and we looked at each other dumbfounded.

'Inspection,' said a voice outside.

We opened the door, and two soldiers with rifles and fixed bayonets came in, followed by an officer. About a dozen policemen were standing outside. This small cabin was packed with three additional people.

Len Chun tried to move towards the door a little bit, and a soldier immediately shouted:

'Stop! Do you want to escape?'

'Why should I escape?'

'Why did you move to the door?'

'Because I wanted a little fresh air.' Len Chun was on the point of fighting with the soldier, but he did his best to suppress his anger.

The officer was more reasonable. He said:

'What is your name? Where do you come from? . . .'

While our suitcases, blankets, covered bundles, baskets and everything were being carefully searched by the two soldiers, the officer was asking us endless questions.

'I am Hsieh Yun Tze, and I am a native of Changsha,' I said.

'And who is she?'

'She is my younger sister.'

'Your younger sister?' He gave I Chin a thorough examination from head to foot, and showed my remark was not convincing. 'But she is taller than you are.'

'Certainly you are joking. There are even children who are taller than their parents.'

Some of the policemen outside laughed.

'Since she is your sister, why is there no family resemblance between you?' Evidently the officer had determined to make trouble for me.

'As our proverb says: "Ten children of one family would have ten different faces." Our faces are not made from one mould. Of course we are not bound to look like each other.'

'How cunning you are!'

I was very angry and was prepared to retort, but Len Chun touched me secretly to give me a warning, and I suppressed my anger.

'What are you doing here with these two young ladies?' he turned to ask Len Chun.

'They are my cousins. They live in Hankow. They came to Changsha to see my mother and stayed with her for two weeks, and I am now seeing them off on their return journey.'

I could see that Len Chun was suppressing his anger. He realised that when a student meets with a soldier, there is no reasoning, and now especially, when we were escaping from our families, we should be more submissive.

'Where are you working?'

'At the Salt Office.' Len Chun immediately showed them his badge and they were satisfied, and they had to walk out rather reluctantly.

Crossing the threshold the officer said rather sarcastically:

'When you are sitting in a room with two young cousins of the opposite sex you should not shut the door. It looks very fishy.'

We were nearly choked with rage, but on realising that we were two runaways we said no more.

'The first difficulty is now over.' I Chin shivered and heaved a deep sigh of relief. 'I was so afraid.'

'I was not afraid at all. As has been said before, the worst could only be death, and death is not so terrible!' I remarked.

'Good, that is the spirit! If you have daring and spirit, and are prepared to sacrifice everything to fight against bad influences, you are sure to have victory. I hope you will not be disturbed by set-backs, which you are bound to encounter, but will continue fighting.' Len Chun's words were like a lecture which was deeply impressed on our minds.

'Mr. Len Chun, thank you very much for the trouble you have taken to see us off. Now it is almost ten o'clock, when the curfew will be enforced. You had better hurry home.' I urged him to go, but he seemed to be still worrying about us.

'I had better stay a little longer with you, in case other people may come and make trouble for you.'

'Never mind now. As soon as the curfew is enforced nobody except the police and the soldiers will be allowed to go about, and as we have already passed their inspection we are all right. What I feared was people from our families, and now they will not be able to come out.'

At three minutes to ten Len Chun had reluctantly to bid us farewell.

'I hope all will be well with you. Write to me immediately you arrive at Hankow.'

'Of course, but also you should have a look at to-morrow's papers, in case there would be anything about us there, then you need not wait for a letter from Hankow.'

We all laughed uneasily.

Chapter XXXIX

THE NIGHT OF TERROR

Night came ; a dark night, without even starlight.

Midnight passed. No sound whatever came from the shore. Because of the curfew law in force, we could not even hear the cries of the refreshment sellers on the wharf. The whole city of Changsha was wrapped in darkness, except for a few sparkles of dim electric light, which seemed to look miserable to us. All the sailors and passengers on board the steamer 'Tung Ting Maru' were now fast asleep. The only people who were awake were the two passengers in cabin No. 13, that was myself and I Chin, and perhaps an elderly lady who was coughing, and a baby who broke out into crying.

The wind dashed the waves against the bows, making a sound similar to a distant bell.

All the heat was gone. The evening breeze was as refreshing and cooling as if it were an autumn night. I tossed about in my berth, sticking my head out and looking at I Chin who was also tossing in the berth above me.

'I Chin, are you still awake? Why don't you go to sleep?'

'I cannot sleep. I am always afraid that my family will follow me.'

'What, are you crying again? I told you to cry is useless. Since you have determined to escape, you must cast fear aside. You are crying because you are thinking of your home. What is there to think about?'

'No, I am not thinking of my home. I was only worried in case I should be dragged back home again, when I would be forced into a marriage to which I object. Then my life would be ruined.'

'I Chin, they must have thought you were spending a night with your aunt. If they had known you were going on board a ship, they would have been here long ago.'

'Perhaps they might think that I was going away by train. I left my home about three o'clock in the afternoon, and they could take the night express to Hankow, waiting for me there.'

'In that case they will be waiting for you at the wharf in Hankow.'

We really seemed to be afloat on a tiny, lonely boat in an extensive sea in the dark. After one wave had swept over us, another followed immediately. There was no light whatever on us, and we could not see our direction or how dangerous it was. At this moment I Chin felt that a thousand knives were cutting her heart. She was a girl barely sixteen, and had been rather spoiled by her grandmother who loved her very dearly. She went to an art school at thirteen, and soon became the best student in that school. Two years later there came to her school a young teacher who was very handsome and talented, and the poor girl fell for him immediately. It was a one-sided love, for as the girl dare not reveal her feelings he was unaware of her love. Very soon he joined the Revolution, and was killed somewhere in Honan.

Since then I Chin had decided to follow in his steps and devote her life to the Revolution in memory of him. Her family learned of her queer ways, and wanted to marry her off to the boy who was betrothed to her when they were only babies. I Chin at first tried to commit suicide by jumping into the river, but she was rescued. Again and again she wrote me asking me to take her away from her home, and she was only too glad when I came to Changsha and offered her the only opportunity she would ever have, to go to Shanghai with me. This time, if she could leave Changsha all would be well for her. She was prepared for any sacrifice.

I was very grateful to my friend Len Chun. Although he was only indirectly a friend of mine, we were as good as brother and sister who would help each other in times of distress. Not only were our ideas the same, but we were also fellow sufferers from the same old system.

Slowly I Chin fell asleep and all was silent again.

'Ah, mother, I am not going home. I had rather die!' I Chin cried loudly in nightmare.

I hurried to her and pressed my hand over her mouth.

'I—I am afraid. Look—look at the window. Don't you see my mother has come?' She sat up, wiping her tears with one hand and pointing at the window with the other.

'No, there is nobody there. Everybody is asleep, you mustn't waken them. It was only your imagination.'

Although I was trying to comfort her, I was a little bit startled myself. I had already glanced at the window, and seemed to see a dark shape moving outside. Might it be that my eldest brother had come to get me back, or was it really somebody from her home? This suspicion, this terror was always in my mind, though outwardly I tried to be calm.

After I had made I Chin go to sleep again, I walked outside the cabin for a breath of fresh air.

'Hey, what are you doing!' A cross and angry voice caused me to step back. I found that I was treading on somebody who was sleeping outside my cabin.

'I am sorry,' I said quietly.

'You have been seeing devils! Don't you see that you have been treading on my head.' The man was very angry.

'I am extremely sorry.   I didn't see you.'

'Are you blind? You should look before you tread.'

The night became silent again, except for the sound of the waves in the river.

The half-moon was cold and lonesome hanging in the western sky. A few twinkling stars could be seen, and the atmosphere was very eerie. The night wind, although very gentle, was blowing incessantly upon me, and l felt I could not withstand it. If my eldest brother came on board, what could I do? Jump into the river, or run away? Drowning myself was too great a sacrifice, I would not do it. To run away was impossible. Not only would the police be on his side, but even the passengers on board would stop me. What could I do?

'Hey, what are you standing there for?' This question was so sudden that I was frightened to death. A big dark shape appeared before me. I looked carefully and recognised the purser who had sold me the tickets.

'The room is too stuffy. I came out for a breath of fresh air.' I forced a smile for him. 'It is cool outside.'

'But why didn't your sister come and keep you company?'

'A little girl like her doesn't mind being in a stuffy room. She is fast asleep.'

He bade me good night, but I became suspicious. I returned to my cabin immediately and shut the door.

Bang! Bang! Bang! Bang! Another series of loud knocks came on our door.

'Oh, my mother! I am afraid,' cried I Chin.

The knocks became more loud and rapid.

'Who is there?' I asked calmly.

'I want somebody by the name of Wong,' the voice outside replied.

'No, you are wrong. There is nobody of that name here.'

'You had better open the door and let me have a look.'

'Why should I open the door for you?'

'Open the door, please.'

In order to avoid further trouble I decided to open the door. Two men flashed their torches all over the room. I was frightened to death, but they smiled and said:

'We are very sorry to disturb you. We were mistaken.'

'Never mind. It's all right.'

They went away and I shut the door again.

'Sister Min, you can see I am wet through with perspiration. My head has become cold and my breath stopped for a while. I thought they were coming for me.' I Chin was still panting. I gave her a sad smile.

Alas, even the grass and the trees were as dangerous to us as soldiers. Whatever sound we heard, it was enough to frighten us and make us tremble. I hoped the boat would very soon set sail, otherwise we would never be able to endure the night.

We heard a clicking sound of heavy chains. They were weighing anchor. A pale light slowly came in through the porthole.

'Good! I am happy. Now is the time for us to start.' I held I Chin's head in my arms and kissed her madly. I Chin, too, was shedding tears of joy. 'Now we are free!'

We heard the turning of the big wheels and the repeated sound of the sirens. The water in the river roared as if a thousand soldiers and ten thousand horses were shouting and roaring. The boat turned slowly to the east, and its speed became quicker and quicker. In the twinkling of an eye we were in the middle of the Shiang River.

'Good-bye, good-bye, Changsha!' When the red disc of the sun began to appear above the water in the east, I held I Chin's hand as we sat on deck and welcomed the coming of the dawn and the beginning of our new life.

CHAPTER XL

MORE TERRORS

The 'Tung Ting Maru' steamed for a day and a night before we reached Hankow. There we spent the night at Mon Ton's house. She was a fellow-soldier with me in the Wu Chang days, and had now become the wife of the editor of the paper *Lone Sail*.

The next evening we booked a ticket for one berth in the third-class general cabin for Shanghai. Mon Ton and her husband were not at all well off. They could not afford to buy any fruit to give us for our voyage, and in fact we had to walk from her house to the steamer 'Shui Ho.' This was my first experience of travelling in a big steamer. It was crowded with passengers; even the passage and the deck were full. It seemed to me that in many places men were on top of men, and it was with great difficulty that we found our berth among mountains and seas of men. The smell from the sweating passengers was as strong as ammonia.

'Two people sleeping in one berth? I think you had better buy another one.' A fat steward said this to us with a smile, hoping to do a little business with us. He saw we were tidily dressed and had friends to see us off, and ought to be able to afford to pay a little more. Of course he never dreamt that seven dollars was all we had in the world.

This big general cabin was one of the biggest on board, and there were more than three hundred berths in it. All the berths were in three tiers, and ours was one at the side with a small porthole above it, but it was the lowest berth and in spite of the porthole it was very dark. Our neighbour was a great opium smoker, and the smell made us nearly sick.

'I think you had better go home. The air here is very bad, and we have no room to invite you to sit down.' I urged our friends to go, not only for their sakes but for my own, for I was hoping to have a little rest myself. But they insisted on staying until the time of sailing, so there was nothing for it but to sit uncomfortably on our berth.

The steward came to collect the passage money, and I paid four dollars for that berth.

'We have more passengers than we can cater for in the general cabin. This berth was really my own, but since you ladies wanted it so badly, I have given it up for you. But please understand that it can be let down only at night. During the daytime we have to push it back in order to make room for the people to pass.'

When the steward told us this we were all surprised.

'Where shall we sit in the daytime, then?' my friend Mon Ton demanded of him.

'This is a passage and an important thoroughfare for the stewards to serve the meals. Because we are too crowded we were ordered to make more room by pushing the berths against the wall.'

'Where shall we sit in the daytime, then?'

'Ah, if you ladies want to sit you should buy a second or even a first-class cabin. All the people in the third class, especially in the general cabin, must stand.'

'Do we have to stand until we reach Shanghai?'

'I am sorry, but I cannot help it.'

'Give us our money back. What is the use of such a berth?' Mon Ton's husband insisted that we should go home with them and sail by another boat the next day, but we were resolved that we had better go then. While I Chin was afraid her mother might be coming for her, I was not comfortable in a place like Hankow. Physical suffering was of small consequence to me. As soon as we reached Shanghai all would be well.

The gong sounded and we bade farewell to our friends.

I took out a pillow and a blanket from my travelling basket, and I Chin asked me:

'Such a narrow strip of board, how can it hold two people?'

'Let us try. If it is too narrow, then we shall have to sleep in turns. You sleep for the first half of the night while I sit, then I will sleep during the second half of the night while you sit. That will be the only solution.'

'But where can one sit?'

'On the berth.'

'But you cannot sit here. You will bump your head against the middle berth.' I Chin was really unhappy, but I tried to comfort her.

'Never mind. In any case it will be very hot at night, and I don't think I can possibly sleep at all. The night air will be very fresh, especially on this mighty Yangtze River. We will have a walk on deck to look at the moon.'

True to what I had said, when night came we did not go to sleep, but walked on deck looking at the moon and stars.

The moon was pure, and the landscape on either side of the river was as clear as in the bright day. We saw the distant mountains, rice fields, villages, forests; everything was very clear. The river in the moonlight was like an extensive field covered with gold. The sounds from the engine-room came in unison with that of the waves lapping against the bows of the boat. It was powerful and majestic.

In contrast to these beautiful pictures and harmonious sounds there lay before us everywhere passengers who were no better than refugees. All of them were in rags, and some of the boys were totally naked, while the girls had nothing but a small piece of cloth for their attire. They were seated and prostrated in all kinds of attitudes, and you could hear their loud snores. The moon-beams made their complexions paler than they really were, and gave one a picture of slavery and suppression.

Because I Chin had not slept well for the two previous nights, she went to the berth first, while I lingered on deck, watching the clouds which were racing forward over the stars and the moon. The night was serene. The whole universe was asleep. But one could hear many sounds—of the engine, of the water, the chirruping of insects and the beautiful song of the nightingales coming from the shore. I lingered on deck for a long while before returning to the general cabin.

Long after her turn had expired I Chin was still fast asleep in the berth. I couldn't possibly bear to awaken her, so I crouched into an uncomfortable bundle with my two feet dangling above the ground. I tried to have a little rest, but in ten minutes I felt cramped all over. Strangely enough, however, even in such a position I was soon soundly asleep.

In a very big cotton factory I became a working girl looking after a spinning machine. Suddenly one of the cotton threads broke, and when I tried to join it my hand got caught in the wheels. I drew it back hurriedly and three of my fingers were gone. The white thread became red and I was looking at it dumbfounded when I was knocked on the head by a very heavy club.

'Ayiau!' I shouted aloud, and found the foreman thought I was being lazy and was punishing me.

I awakened immediately from my dream and realised that the old man in the middle berth had dropped his rice bowl accidentally and it had landed on my head, which was protruding out of my berth. Hot blood was indeed flowing, and my clothes became red immediately.

Unwittingly I had cried aloud and wakened all the people around. I Chin too sat up, and the old man got down to wipe my head with his towel. The stewards came running to me, asking me how I felt, but the pain was so great that I could not answer them.

Suddenly I saw a pair of quick dark eyes steadfastly fixed on me, and I was afraid. They belonged to a big dark man who was also a steward, and he searched me from head to foot. At last he scolded the old man very severely, and demanded that he should give up his berth to me because he had wounded me.

'I am very sorry. It was careless of me, but it was not intentional. I hope you will pardon me.' The old man was very apologetic, and I thought he was really not to blame. If I had not protruded my head out of my berth, the accident would never have happened. It was really due to our being too hard up to buy two berths that I had this misfortune. How could I blame other people?

'You have broken this young lady's head. This is very serious.' The dark steward would not let him alone.

I Chin whispered to me:

'The steward is rather strange. He is trying to help you.'

I signed to her to be silent and said to the steward:

'Never mind, I am feeling better now, thank you.'

I was not speaking the truth. Really my wound was as painful as if a hammer were striking me incessantly.

'I will get some ointment for you from the purser. You will soon be better.'

When this strange steward was gone I began to tremble with fear. Why should he be so good to me? Was there any danger?

Soon I Chin went to sleep again, while I, holding my head in both hands, sat up until morning.

The morning meal was served.

The passengers of the third class were only given two meals a day, and they were only coarse rice with nothing to go with it. Just before every meal the steward would bring a pail of muddy water, officially called tea, and that was served to every passenger instead of soup. I went to buy two pieces of salted bean curd to go with the rice, and I Chin thought that was not enough, and asked me why I did not buy some egg and fish. I had to tell her that all the money left in my pocket was three dollars, and from that I had to pay the tip to the steward who was looking after us.

When the second meal was served on that day, the dark steward suddenly appeared before me with two bowls of lovely white refined rice. He also brought a small packet of salted fish and some preserved cabbage.

'We do not need them. Please take them back.' I dare not accept any presents because I was not able to make out why he was so good to us.

'Take them, please. They are free of charge.' He put them down and went away. I was told that he was a steward from the first class.

'I hope he has not put poison in these things.' After eating them I Chin began to have misgivings.

'Foolish child, why should he try to poison us?'

In spite of our misgivings, we enjoyed the meal very much. Not a grain of rice was left.

Chapter XLI

DELIVERANCE

Night, fearsome night, approached again.

I Chin was as drowsy as a sleeping bug. Before it was very dark she was sound asleep again. When I wanted a little sleep, no matter how tired I was I felt I could not bear to get her out of the berth to spend the night as a night watcher. At last, because my head was so painful, I had to recline beside her, and very soon I found she was sleeping on top of me. Her legs were as heavy as bags of stone pressed on my breast. I wakened to find I was covered with perspiration. Then the opium smoker began his night smoking, and because the smell was so bad I had to go on deck for some fresh air.

Strange, in the place which was a passage in the daytime there stretched a bamboo couch. As I saw nobody was there, I sat on it.

'I am sorry. I saw there was no one about so I sat here temporarily.' When I saw the dark steward coming towards me I stood up and made this apology to him.

'I knew you were suffering last night, so I specially prepared this bamboo couch for you to rest. I wanted to tell you before but you were asleep when I visited you. Now you had better sleep here.' His attitude made me more suspicious than ever, but as I looked at him carefully he seemed to have a kind face, and furthermore, I seemed to have seen that face somewhere before.

How foolish! This was my first trip on this steamer. How could I have seen him before?

'No, I don't want to sleep. You can take it away.' I pulled a long face and said this to him.

'Perhaps you do not dare to sleep. Never mind, you can sit on it.' He smiled at me.

When I sat down he called me by the name of Comrade Hsieh. He said that he had met me at Shan-Lin, and asked me whether I could remember him at all.

'No, you are mistaken. I have never been at Shan-Lin and my name is not Hsieh.'

'Please do not be suspicious. When I saw you yesterday I began to remember your face. That is why I dared to offer you a little rice to-day. Please do not be afraid. Nobody would recognise you.'

'No, you are mistaken. I do not understand what you say, and I am sure you must have taken me for somebody else.'

I thought he might be a spy trying to drag me into a confession, but he told me that he was the foreman of the jury during the trial of the three prisoners in Shan-Lin district, which we passed on our westward march. His name was Chien Yuan Chi.

All the clouds of doubt were gone now, and I remembered him very distinctly. His dark eyes when he appealed to the crowd for confirmation of the verdict of the court, and his commanding voice were still fresh in my mind. Yes, I certainly remembered seeing him before, but how could he remember me, I being only one of many women soldiers who passed through that district?

'You were on the night watch, and I heard you had some trouble with one of those rogues. I could never forget your face once I had seen it.'

We soon became fast friends.

'My work in Shan-Lin was known to very few people. When I asked leave from the steamer, I gave as a pretext that my mother was dead and I had to see to the funeral and the burial. Now that the Revolution has been suppressed, I had to come back and resume my old job. As I always did my duty, they had nothing to say against me, although they might have suspicions of me.'

'I hope you will tell me more about what happened when we left there. Have the masses of Shan-Lin and Hung-Ko suffered very much?'

At that time I felt as though those places were my native land, and I was very anxious to know what had happened to the progressive young men, and particularly those young women who were working for the emancipation of their sisters.

'Alas, it was tragic!' He heaved a deep sigh. 'When you first came to us all the people thought that they would be delivered for ever, and all the rogues who had been oppressing them brought to justice. But within one month they were thrown into hell again, and it was much worse than before. The war lords came back, and without any reason they shot all those girls who had cut their hair, and machine-gunned and killed over a thousand

farmers and working people. Of course, there might be many real
Communists among them, many who were mortal enemies of the
war lords, but nine-tenths of them were just innocent country
people. Those rogues who had escaped us went back when they
heard that the Revolutionary Army was withdrawn. They immediately acted as henchmen for the war lords, and killed many
Revolutionary young people who once worked for the welfare of
the whole community.'

When I heard this, a thousand indescribable feelings entered
my mind. I thought I had suffered much, but it seemed to me that
what these people met with was a thousand times worse than mine.
I then asked what happened to those women who were working
that night in the office of the Women's League at Hung-Ko. His
answer was:

'They have all become martyrs too.'

'Alas, who would have thought that the political change would
be so rapid as to make our dreams of the Revolution appear like
a passing cloud!'

'Do not be pessimistic. The new world is in the making. A
great epoch is coming, and we must be prepared for it.'

He said this to comfort me and, I think, to comfort himself also.
When we saw that somebody was coming, we departed immediately.

'I Chin, let me tell you some good news. That dark steward
was somebody whom I knew, so he was very attentive to us. You
need not be afraid now. He will see that we are safe.' I shook and
awakened I Chin and gave her this marvellous news. She almost
shouted: 'That is admirable!'

'Don't talk so loud, you may waken other people.'

This was like a glass of sweet dew given to somebody who had
been travelling for days in the desert.

The weather in these summer days was very changeable.
Suddenly all those people who were sleeping outside in the
moonlight with bare backs, rushed inside. Torrents of rain were
pouring down, and the children began to cry very bitterly.
Immediately I thought of the rich passengers, who would not be
in the least affected by this sudden change of the elements. They
would still be sleeping soundly in their comfortable berths
without any disturbance.

The atmosphere in this general cabin was almost unbearable,

but after three days and three nights our sufferings were ended. When the boat was sailing into Woo Sung port I, like the lone swan, having flown over the Pacific Ocean, the Himalaya Mountains and indeed over the whole world, had arrived somewhere. But where was my destination? Shanghai was only a temporary stepping-stone for me. I was a wanderer without home.

I looked intently on the wild rolling waves of the Yangtze River. The roar of the water seemed to me to be a new revelation.

Flow on like this mighty river. To go forward is the only way to find your final destination. No matter what hardships you are going to meet with, shoaly sandbanks or dangerous rocks, you will overcome them all and will bring new life to everything that you meet!

The siren sounded like a bugle call. We drew in at E Wo wharf. There on the bank of the Woo Sung River were motor-cars, tramcars, carriages and buses moving very busily before a background of high chimneys and factories and lofty buildings. Shanghai is a sample of western civilisation. While the rich people spend their millions here seeking for pleasure, I could hear labourers who were working as stevedores on the wharf singing aloud, 'Yo-ho, yo-ha.' This is their song, this is their groan and their war-cry. It will awaken mankind.

'Here is Shanghai. I will take you to your friends,' Comrade Chien, the steward, said to me with a smile. He carried my luggage with him, and full of hope and a sense of deliverance, together with an acrid smell of sweat about us, we walked towards the Bund.

THE END